GATHERED AND SENT

GATHERED AND SENT

The Mission of Small Church Communities Today

Bernard J. Lee, S.M.
Michael A. Cowan

A Revision and Expansion of
Conversation, Risk, and Conversion

Foreword by Thomas H. Groome

Paulist Press
New York/Mahwah, N.J.

Cover and book design by Lynn Else

Library of Congress Cataloging-in-Publication Data

Lee, Bernard J., 1932–
    Gathered and sent : the mission of small church communities today /
Bernard J. Lee, Michael A. Cowan.
      p. cm.
    Rev. ed. of: Conversation, risk, and conversion / Michael Cowan. c1997.
    ISBN 0-8091-4132-9 (alk. paper)
    1. Basic Christian communities—United States. 2. Sociology, Christian
(Catholic)—United States. I. Cowan, Michael. II. Cowan, Michael.
Conversation, risk, and conversion. III. Title.
    BX2347.72.U6 C68 2003
    262'.26—dc21
                                    2003003549

Published by Paulist Press
997 Macarthur Boulevard
Mahwah, New Jersey 07430

www.paulistpress.com

Printed and bound in the
United States of America

Contents

Small Christian Communities
and the Future Church

The church of the future will be one built from below by basic com-munities as a result of free initiative and association.

The basic communities...will have to develop for the most part out of existing parishes...This does not exclude the fact that a basic community has its own pronounced character, gives itself a certain structure and (if you like to use the term) constitution, and that it really demands from its freely associated members something which goes completely beyond what a parish-ioner today has to do for the ordinary parish...

We should make every effort not to hold up this development, but to promote it and direct it...The church will exist only by being constantly renewed by a free decision of faith...in the midst of a secular world...for the church cannot be a real factor in secular history except as sustained by the faith on the part of human beings...Basic communities will in fact emerge from below, even though it will be a call from the gospel and the message of the church coming out of the past.

Karl Rahner
The Shape of the Church to Come

Foreword

New Hope for a Church of "Holy Order"

The concerns of bishops about collegiality in the larger Catholic Church are echoed in the concerns of many Christians about participative structures in their more immediate settings. The participative impulse is large and clear in how small church communities organize themselves and frequently how they relate to the parish. In the Papal Exhortation *Ecclesia in Asia*, following upon the synod there, Pope John Paul II writes that "each local church should become what the synod fathers called a 'participatory church'….In this context and drawing upon their pastoral experience, the synod fathers underline the value of basic ecclesial communities…." (par. 25). Small communities in the U.S. Catholic Church are beginning to pave the way, but the terrain doesn't lend itself to easy road-making. The resistances to a true participatory élan are deep.

A favorite Catholic code word for how the church puts its life together is "hierarchy," but so much depends on how that gets interpreted. Remember that hierarchy once had a very different meaning than the one presumed in common parlance today. From the Greek *hier-arche*, its literal sense is "holy order." But rather than a tiered system of command, with the upper echelons handing down orders to the levels below, "hierarchy" originally meant getting people to work well together. As such, it is the opposite of *anarche*—anarchy. A Christian community realizes such "holy order" as all its members participate and work together effectively within, and in its mission to the world, contributing according to their gifts and receiving according to their needs. This sense of things is reflected, for example, in the directive from the Second Vatican Council that "all the faithful be led to that full, conscious, and active participation in

1

liturgical celebrations which is demanded by the very nature of the liturgy" (*Constitution on the Liturgy*, Par. 14).

It seemed eminently consistent with the preaching of Jesus for the early church to call itself to hierarchy. As Paul had imagined, it should function as the Body of Christ in the world, with all the members included and appreciated, all the gifts welcomed and engaged, all the parts working together in "holy order." Alas, this is not what hierarchy came to mean for the church's structural style, nor for its way of doing theology.

When the disciples were jostling for who "would be the greatest," Jesus warned "it must not be that way among you." He made it very explicit that they should never "lord it over" people; true greatness is simply the willingness to serve (Mark 9:34 and 10:42–45). Later, reiterating that "the greatest" in his community would be servant leaders, Jesus urged disciples to "call no one father" (Matt 23:9); the context clearly implies an egalitarian sentiment. Yet no institution seems more hierarchically ordered in the top-down chain-of-command sense than the Catholic expression of his church.

And as might be expected, a similar top-down model emerged in how the church does theology. One could tell a long-winded story here but the upshot was that theology gradually became the exclusive preserve of highly trained specialists who, it was assumed, would work at theoretical heights to hand down what people need to know and do in faith. Indeed the church will always need and be well served by experts trained in the original languages, hermeneutical tools, and conceptual patterns needed to mine the depths and richness of scripture and Christian tradition. But such expertise should not reduce the other 99.9 percent of the Christian people to silence and theological dependence. On the contrary and to incarnate their faith, all Christians and their communities must engage in bringing "faith to understanding" and beyond that to daily life. Every Christian must learn to bring life to faith, and faith to life— to "do" theology on their feet.

So for the church to struggle toward "holy order," enabling its people to work well together, welcoming and nurturing all the gifts to function like a healthy body, is ever its vocation and horizon. And for each disciple and community to be agents in faith rather than dependents, to be players rather than spectators, will require a very different mode of theologizing than experts explaining things to everyone else.

The church is forever and always in transformation. It says of itself that it is always *semper reformanda*, always in need of conversion. Into the creative breach between what has been and what might be, there now enters this powerful book by Bernard Lee and Michael Cowan, *Gathered and Sent: The Mission of Small Church Communities Today*. If we take seriously and practice their proposal, we will be well on our way to some real "holy order" in the church's life and thought.

In this revised and expanded version of *Conversation, Risk, and Conversion*, Michael and Bernard renew and deepen the call to become a church that realizes itself from the bottom up. They lend the scriptural and theological warrant for what is emerging as the "small Christian community" movement, and reflecting on empirical data from the life of such communities—with nigh fifty thousand now functioning within the United States—they deepen the story and stretch the vision of this movement, surely one inspired by the Holy Spirit.

The risen Christ reassembled the first "small Christian community" on a hillside in Galilee, only to send them out to carry on his mission to the ends of the earth (see Matt 28:16–20). In Christian faith, community is always for mission. So Bernard and Michael make the clarion call here that such communities must have their own inner spiritual life that sustains their members in faith and likewise a public mission that brings Christian faith to the social structures and cultural contexts of their time and place. Far from being "salvation clubs" designed "for members only," these small communities must function like a sacrament of God's reign in the world.

Likewise, the authors propose a mode of doing theology within such communities that is marked by conversation and active participation by all. This will be a "theology of praxis"—a practical theology—in that people reflect together on their whole lives, personal and social, in the light of Christian faith in order to enhance their living faith for the life of the world. The essential dynamic of such theology is community conversation with the intent of bringing Christian faith and daily life together as living faith. While one could readily favor such a proposal in theory, realizing it in practice poses great challenges in our individualized world and hierarchical-ized church. To begin with, we need to relearn the art of conversa-tion, with all that good conversation entails. Would-be practitioners will find great practical wisdom here.

To follow the proposals of this prophetic text will surely mark a new day for "holy order" in the church and its way of doing the-ology. And wouldn't it be a gospel-like reversal if what is sometimes experienced as a liability could be reclaimed as a great asset to the church in becoming what it should be, a sacrament of God's reign in the world? Many seeds of such hope have been buried in the tra-dition but are raised up again today by small church communities as so well reflected in this moving text, a gift to us all.

Thomas H. Groome
Boston College, January 2002

1

Small Church Communities:
Long Ago and Once Again—A Church Becoming

Introduction

Small communities are perhaps not the future of the Catholic Church in the world. But it is unlikely that any future church will not bear their mark, and significantly so. That this is a worldwide phenomenon, not called into existence by any institutional voice, and not orchestrated by anyone anyplace, suggests strongly that the unpredictable Spirit of God may be up to something.

In this book we will be pastorally probing the experience of these small communities in the U.S. Catholic Church. This phenomenon goes by many names. In our book *Dangerous Memories* we often spoke of intentional Christian communities (ICCs), because we felt that very deliberate intentionality was an element of membership in any true community. The language in this country shifted to small Christian communities (SCCs), and then to small church communities (still SCCs). The latter one is especially loaded. It can institutionally co-opt the spontaneity of the emergence of SCCs, or it can stake out a claim for the churchhood of SCCs. Because *small church communities* names the critical articulation between these communities and the larger church, we will often name them this way.

We will begin with a description of SCCs in the U.S. church based upon a three-year study of them funded by a Lilly Endowment grant to the Loyola Institute for Ministry in New Orleans. It was designed and carried out by a team of theologians and a team of research experts (four sociologists and one anthropologist) who have published a detailed report on the study, *The*

Catholic Experience of Small Christian Communities (New York/ Mahwah, N.J.: Paulist Press, 2000).

We will also review the notion of "dangerous memories," borrowed from Johannes Metz, because it seems more and more appropriate as the SCC phenomenon expands. Then, indebted especially to the work of Hans-Georg Gadamer, we will suggest "conversation" as a metaphor for the structure of Christian life and see the etymological connection between conversation and conversion, especially as these operate in SCC experience. An actual conversation in a small church community in Nairobi will serve as an example. The kind of conversation we are describing leads us headlong into the bright light of God's intentions for us so that God's reign might increasingly take hold. We conclude the chapter with an overview of the rest of the book.

SCCs in the U.S. Catholic Church

When regular church attendance has dropped from 75–80 percent in 1965 to 32 percent (Lee, 2000, 60), it is certainly worthwhile asking what draws a large number of U.S. Catholics to put in several hours every week or two over and beyond Sunday Eucharist, when parishes do not ordinarily ask or invite this. In our research we wanted to know what kind of people join SCCs, why they do it, what they do when they gather, and what difference it makes.

To begin with, there are minimally 37,000 SCCs. We know areas where our count was incomplete and reckon that the number has continued to grow in the years since the research was completed. We would guess the number at 45,000–50,000.

About 65 percent of them are largely Euro-American communities, usually with parish connections. About 20 percent are Hispanic, and 13 percent charismatic. A small percentage are on college and university campuses, but we know that our count there is incomplete. About 1 percent are Eucharist-centered communities or have a connection, either as a community or through its members, with Call to Action.

Except for the Hispanic communities, members are a little better educated and a little more affluent than the general Catholic population. Half of Hispanic SCC members say that their community members are also their primary social group, suggesting that the Hispanic SCC may at times be part of their inculturation.

The average number of members in a community is thirteen adults, eight women and five men, and often children. Some, of course, are much larger, and others quite small. About three-fourths of the members are 40 years old and older. Preliminary data on college campuses suggests interest on the part of young adults, but they are not in parish-connected groups in very large numbers. SCCs are not so regular a part of parish life that young people can easily move into them after leaving the college or university. Whether they would or not is another question. But making it possible is sound pastoral agenda.

There are two major reasons why people join SCCs, neither of which is any surprise. They are looking for more religious nurture than the parish is providing. This is not a judgment on parish life. The kind of nurture that people's religious sensibilities receive in SCCs is not possible in parish life at-large. The second reason for joining is a hunger for community with relational depth. In *Habits of the Heart*, Robert Bellah and colleagues address the strength of individualism in American culture that makes community difficult because it militates against commitments that tie one down. Those very same dynamics create a sort of cultural loneliness that makes us hanker for community even as we meet it with reluctance. Robert Wuthnow's research suggests, in *Sharing the Journey*, that four out of every ten Americans now belong to some kind of small group. We think of Paul when he encountered Athenians with religious hungers who were worshipping the unknown God, and Paul said, "I know that God. Let me tell you…" Perhaps it is time for Catholic experience to say something similar: "You hunger for community yet fear it. Let me tell you about a magnificent reality called the body of Christ. It takes the fear out of it."

Most SCCs gather every week or every second week, and most of them gather in members' homes. Prayer is always part of the experience. In most communities, major time is spent with scripture, especially in the effort to make connections with their own lived experience. In our judgment, this is where the "magic" is: people's religious interests and interpersonal community interests come together when real life is in intimate dialogue with scripture. In chapter 3 we will return again to the SCC retrieval of the Word's church-making power. Strengthening a herald ecclesiology (in terms of the Dulles models of the church) may be among the better gifts that SCCs are making to the church-at-large, a linked response to both *Dei verbum* and the people of God ecclesiology of *Lumen gentium*. We are not suggesting that this is a deliberate theological agenda, only that some fine instincts are at work. Perhaps the Holy Spirit's?

The research asked SCC members what kind of impact their community experience had on their lives. We might borrow a term from the Latin American tradition: *conscientization*. SCC members regularly say that their community experience has increased their participation in both church life and civil life. They become more aware of their responsibility beyond their immediate concerns. But this is not without a struggle. When asked to name their concerns, over 80 percent of community members named "helping others," and over 20 percent named political issues. But when asked if they engaged in activities related to these concerns, only 39 percent of the largest type of SCC said they did so, and 8 percent named actual political involvement. There is a wide gap between expressed concern for larger social issues and concrete responsiveness to those concerns. We think that a lot of cultural factors play into this gap phenomenon, for example, individualism, and the perception that religion is a private matter and doesn't belong in conversations about economics or politics.

In the U.S. Catholic population at large, there is very skimpy knowledge of the magnificent body of the church's social teaching. It is rarely brought into homilies and sermons in parishes. The major lectionary-based publications for SCCs do not with any regularity access the church's social teaching. Perhaps even more intimidating is the challenge to act effectively on issues: when we know what an issue is, how can we have any impact on the situation? One of our goals in this book is to address the essential connections between any Christian's inner life and his or her presence to the outside world. We also believe that the distinction between *works of mercy* (immediate responses to critical human need) and *works of justice* (critiquing and challenging economic and political systems and structures) is useful. Both are requisite modes of redemptive presence to a wounded world. But if all our energy goes into works of mercy (which admittedly is a less complex response), that can deepen the problem because the dysfunctional system responsible for many immediate needs is not addressed. Uncritically tending their victims over and over can empower unjust systems to endure because someone keeps picking up the pieces.

The other need which the study surfaced as deserving of focused pastoral formation is the area of leadership. A common pattern for a community is to move around to different members' homes, and someone from the guest home is the leader for that gathering. Continuity between concerns expressed in one gathering and the next is often nonexistent. Leadership does not mean that someone takes charge, but it does mean a consistent way in which people's gifts in a community are identified and invited to help the community be and do what it decides it wants to be and do. We will return to this important matter in chapter 5, concerning a community's inner life.

Dangerous Memories

When we first addressed the experience of small Christian communities in our book, *Dangerous Memories: House Churches and Our American Story*, we borrowed the expression "dangerous memories" from the work of Johannes Metz. When we remember that things were other than they are now, and that they were holy and right when they were like that, we suddenly realize that they could also be different than they are now, and be holy and right. Those memories often feel like a "danger" because they make us face the fragility and mutability of the world which we know well and in which we are relatively comfortable. That realization relativizes the present moment—any present moment. Metz says that such memories are dangerous because they break through the canon of the prevailing structures of plausibility and have certain subversive features. They are like dangerous and incalculable visitations from the past. They are memories...with a future content (Metz, 1980, 109–10).

The notion that small Christian communities are rooted in memories with a future content that endangers the status quo has been appealing to our readers and our friends in many workshops and retreats, because it basically rings true. There is drama in the expression "dangerous memories," but it is more than a showpiece. We squirm with the demands it makes, and we smile at the invitation to remake the face of the earth, a vocation we have because we are children of Spirit.

As we began to use the metaphor of conversation to think once again about the character of the small Christian community, we recalled that Hans-Georg Gadamer, who pressed "conversation" into metaphorical service, also reminded us that only those who are willing to put their presumptions at risk can engage in true conversation. We may not change our minds, but we cannot genuinely have confronted otherness and be utterly the same.

In these pages we reassert the intuition laid out in *Dangerous Memories* that small Christian communities are part of a very important conversation in the church today in which participants are beginning to consider taking risks on behalf of the reign of God and the people of God. There is risk indeed. For those of us who know that we live in a world at risk and a church at risk, this is a conversation in which we belong. What we risk by participating is conversion.

Important conversations about life and faith happen often in small Christian communities, but occur far more rarely in the more traditional forms of gathering that have characterized Catholic life. It is the dynamic of the small group, and especially of the small groups that are communities, that makes this important kind of conversation more likely to happen. There were conversations in the early house churches that have not occurred regularly since Christian communities lost their marginal status with the conversion of Constantine and the mid-fourth-century assimilation of Christianity into the dominant culture. The conversations that reconstitute us are the daily interactions between friends, family members, and community members. They are conversations between Christian communities and the larger worlds that constitute their social environment. They are conversations between God and the people of God.

Any conversation between faith and experience is an on-the-spot doing of theology. This is a regular activity in SCCs, although one they are not aware of. When asked in the research whether their communities engaged in theological reflection, less than a fourth said they did. But when the communities were visited, dialogue between experience and faith was one of the things they did most consistently and deliberately. We had not asked the "theological reflection" question in a way that reflected what we really wanted to know. Our suspicion is that most respondents to the research questions interpreted "theological reflection" as a discussion of a theologian's work or an official church text. And such discussion did not happen often in the small communities we studied.

When people who are serious about their faith try to make informed connections between faith and experience, they are doing grassroots theology. SCC members might not think of themselves as having a theological calling, but that is indeed what they do. They are looking for ultimate meaning from which to live. One of the tasks of academic theology is to receive this grassroots theological reflection, engage it more systematically in conversation with the larger church's mission to collaborate with God's intentions for the world, and help keep it grounded in the traditions that have clarified the church's *raison d'etre* over many centuries. The grassroots or practical theological reflection that ordinary people do to keep their lives oriented to something ultimate is theology in its primary sense; academic theology proper is secondary, to challenge and support grassroots theological reflection.

Conversation and Conversion

Conversation is the root metaphor for this book. It is no etymological fluke that conversation and conversion have the same roots in the Latin. Throughout our lives our conversations change us and move us and often convert us. The root connection between conversion and conversation is more than fun with words. The etymological connection tells an important truth. It tells us a story about our humanness. And our divineness.

Verto, vertere, versi, versus are the Latin forms of the verb "turn." Adding *con-* makes the verb mean "to turn with…" or "to go in a new direction with…" It takes on a dialogic sense. We say in English, for example, that our friends "were conversing with each other."

In Latin a noun can be made from the final part of the verb, here *conversus*. The noun from *conversus* is *conversio*, or "conversion." Conversion always involves interaction with another or with others, or simply with otherness. It is not a simple, individual "turn around." It is a turn we take in the company of others.

Latin lends itself to creating a new verb with a more intensive meaning, again using the last part of the verb. Thus from *conversus* we also get the new intensified verb *converso, conversare, conversavi, conversatus*. And when you make an intensified noun out of an intensified verb, the last part of the verb, *conversatus*, is once more pressed into service, and the new noun is *conversatio*, or "conversation" in English. Intensified conversation and conversion are connected at their roots.

That conversion and conversation are related in meaning and etymology is no superficial intuition. "We say that we 'conduct' a conversation, but the more genuine a conversation is, the less its conduct lies within the will of either partner. Thus a genuine conversation is never the one that we wanted to conduct. Rather it is generally more correct to say that we fall into conversation, or even that we become involved in it. The way one word follows another, with the conversation taking its own twists and reaching its own conclusion, may well be conducted in some way, but we are far less the leaders of it than the led. No one knows what will 'come out' of a conversation. Understanding or its failure is like an event that happens to us" (Gadamer, 1990, 383).

Gadamer says that true conversation always puts conversants at risk, because you cannot truly converse without allowing for the possibility that your assumptions about life might be changed in the process. Put people together in genuine community where conversation allows them to participate in one another's lives *(koinonia)*, and throw the Christ-event in as a conversation partner *(kerygma)*, and *ekklesia* is born. Church happens.

Conversation is our word for the way of living which lies at the heart of both the inner and public life of SCCs. Conversion is what happens whenever authentic conversation occurs. Community is the place where conversation continually holds the possibility of conversion.

Conversation as a Metaphor for Engaged Living

A metaphor is a way of revealing the truth, when something about one thing is truly like another thing. We are all familiar with the literal use of "conversation" in our culture: two or more people speaking and listening to each other with a degree of genuine mutuality in their dialogue. The metaphor can be stretched to let us conceive of conversation with a text, a tradition, or even with a social system.

It is a metaphor to talk about our conversation with a text, since conversation usually means something that goes on between people. But often a metaphor that took us in one direction turns around and surprises us with a new metaphor when it comes back to us. We usually think about reading a text, but we can also tell a metaphorical truth by noting that we learn to "read" each other's lives. We read our tradition. We read our social systems.

We begin with some of the most obvious literal meanings of good conversation, then expand the metaphor to illuminate the life of a community.

Every act of human communication involves reading and being read. We interpret and we are interpreted. We never have unmediated or uninterpreted access to the experience of others or even of ourselves. Every perception of others or ourselves is an interpretation. In our lives together there are no uninterpreted facts. Dialogue between people is but one instance of the back-and-forth movement of questions and answers. We dialogue with our church, with our community, always interpreting as we do. This is a political act, because it is about how people live and work together in the same city (or same church, or same family, or same friendship). *Polis* is the Greek word for city, the place where people come for common purpose. Here they have to work things out, often in compromise, to achieve a common purpose. Being political is always part of being human, no less in church than in the city.

The meanings of conversation just described are operative whether we address the relationship between community members or between the community and the larger church, the community and the neighborhood or city, or the community and the nation's economy.

People, and maybe religious people even more so, are often haunted by a false "nicety norm" to systematically avoid any topic of conversation that might touch politics or religion, and to keep well hidden all of the things that in fact divide us. The rules of authentic conversation are to help us avoid this dysfunctional kind of avoidance. We will, therefore, consider briefly the rules of the game, remembering that conversation is our working metaphor both for life in small Christian communities and in their interactive life in the larger world.

We are all familiar with tensions that arise from the encounters between experience and tradition, for example, when young adults argue with the inherited wisdom of their forebears, or when Catholics argue with the inherited wisdom of theirs. Many times the inherited wisdom calls our current interpretation into question and its challenge is right. Other times the inherited wisdom refuses to learn a new wisdom from a new experience for a new time. The dialectic between experience and tradition is as fierce as it is transformative.

The practical fruit of mutual meetings of any kind, and therefore of SCCs, is the difference they make for the subsequent directions of our lives. Possible futures, ways that our lives might unfold, inevitably surface in authentic dialogue, in the form of invitation and confrontation. Those possibilities then await our response. They may appear as a result of momentous, once-in-a-lifetime meetings which later seem to have changed the shape of our lives. Even more important for most of us are our ongoing exchanges with the conversation partners named friend, spouse, neighbor, community member, and church—and, yes, even (or especially) enemy. Within the dialogical web of these sacred everyday relations, possible futures are always taking form.

Conversations That Create Us

In his influential book *Philosophy and the Mirror of Nature*, Richard Rorty says that he does not understand philosophy to be an articulation of timeless, indisputable principles, but rather an ongoing conversation in any culture about what matters most. And he says that such conversations are so vital that they in fact contribute constitutively to a society's character. They help make it be what it is. We are making a similar claim for SCCs: conversation is a root metaphor for the interpersonal interchanges that are, in fact, a community's concrete reality. We would make the same claim for theology that Rorty makes for philosophy, that it is a conversation of such importance that it contributes to the reality of a community's life and its faith.

We proceed now in our characterization of SCCs to name the major conversations that constitute their life and their conversions, and the risks that occur between conversation and conversion.

Conversation with God

All SCCs embrace prayer. Sometimes the leader (of the community or of that week's ritual) will pray in the name of the community, sometimes all members contribute, sometimes both. SCCs are a place where people pray out loud together. In so doing, they find encouragement for their personal prayer lives throughout the week.

Many communities have the breaking open of God's Word as the centerpiece of their regular gathering. The happy rediscovery of the Bible is familiar to SCCs. They usually follow the lectionary, and they often use materials that provide commentary. Sometimes they incorporate readings from other sources. We call our scriptures God's word because of the belief deep in the Judeo-Christian tradition that God spoke not only once, which those texts record, but speaks still and again through them. When our contemporary encounter with Word meets our lived experience, our grappling together as a community and our action are our speech back to God. With our lives, we hear, take our stand, make decisions, and speak. We are in conversation with God. It constitutes us as community.

Conversation among Community Members

The quality of relationship and support within and among community members is very important to today's SCCs in this country. The data tells us that, in contemporary North American culture, we have a hunger for support groups. In SCCs, the same needs well up even more strongly out of the inexorable logic of baptism. We are, after all, members of one another. We were that already before baptism. In baptism we become by grace what we are through nature, an inner-connectedness that becomes Christ's body, a new being that exacts new behaviors. Paul's tells the house churches in quite specific ways what their conversation together should be like because of who they are.

We do not exist and *then* have relationships. We come out of relationships in the first place. We are interdependent and interconnected family members who share the earth as common home. Christians share the reality of the body of Christ—they are members, one of another. We must be intentional about this. The intentionality is called "commitment," and its object is genuine mutuality.

Conversation beyond the Immediate Community

Members of SCCs are generous and committed. They would not be doing this "something extra" were they not. "Extra" perhaps names the perception that no one has to belong to an SCC—it is chosen. But for many SCC members, the community does not seem extra anymore, but essential. Whether extra or essential, community requires time and energy—in a word, generosity. It is no surprise, therefore, that members of small Christian communities tend to care about social issues.

Many members already have social commitments of one kind or another. They brought these with them when they came to community, and they are appreciated for them. Our experience of SCCs tells us that social energies tend to be present, but that they are rarely named as a community expectation or organized as part of the community's group life.

To be a genuine ecclesial community, a group must be both gathered (attentive to the dynamics of their inner life) and sent (attentive to the dynamics of mission beyond self). SCCs in this country find the dynamics of being gathered easier than the dynamics of mission. This, we believe, is not a matter of generosity, but fallout from U.S. culture and from the rather mistaken presumption that middle-class America is doing well. Hispanic SCCs tend to be more aware of themselves as sent than Anglo SCCs. Culture and economics make the difference.

Overall only a small number of SCCs have explicit commitments to social agenda as a group or as a shared expectation for individual members. Intentional eucharistic SCCs, the SCCs that attend Call to Action, and the SCCs that became part of the research through notices in the *National Catholic Reporter* are more likely to be engaged in activities beyond the immediate group and its concerns. Most of these are not parish connected.

In our experience, communities that try to "pick" a common project rarely find anything that engages the common energies of the whole group. The projects that engage a community profoundly are those that well up out of the community's sustained conversation between its faith and its culture. Issues and priorities become clear only through dialogue—often difficult and tedious dialogue.

While concern for mission does not characterize the majority of SCCs in this country, our experience in workshops, classes, and networking gatherings seems to indicate that social agenda is getting more and more explicit attention. Informed biblical interpretation and skilled social analysis belong essentially to the innards of this conversation. They need not be scholarly, but they must steer wide of biblical fundamentalism and simplistic guesses at social systems, however well intentioned.

Our judgment in this book, for gospel reasons and for sociological reasons, is that SCCs in this country will be just a blip on the screen of ecclesial history rather than an engaging, strong narrative if communities do not have proactive conversation with the world beyond their membership, as well as effective mutual conversation with each other. Gathered *and* sent. The gathering does the sending. The sending calls for gathering.

Conversation with Other Ecclesial Groups

At times people ask, "Don't small Christian communities invite elitism and factions?" That clearly is a possibility. While there have always been factions (*heres* is the Greek word for *faction*), the more small groups there are, the greater the possibility. That needs to be said up front. Paul had to remind the house church communities in Corinth that they didn't belong to Cephas, or to Apollos, but to Christ.

Becoming an idiosyncratic group, floating more or less loose, is antithetical to the reality of church. Part of being truly church is that each church community is in communion with other churches. This church's conversation is in touch with that community's conversation, and with those other churches' communication. Marginal groups especially need lines of communication, and the church's need to hear marginal voices makes cross-conversation fiercely important. At the level of large church, the conversations that bishops have together is essential to church. The Great Councils, like Nicea, Ephesus, Chalcedon, and Vatican II are worldwide, megaconversations.

Practically speaking, the regular gathering of SCC animators or leaders helps parish communities stay in touch with each other's experience, both to teach and learn from one another. Membership in one or more of the national network organizations is another way of staying in touch. The names and addresses at the end of this book indicate networks as well as resources.

A Homiletic Conversation

We want to recount an actual conversation that took place in April 2001 in a house church gathering in Nairobi, Kenya. The bishops of Kenya have placed a high priority on the formation of small church communities. The Catholic Justice and Peace Commission publishes a booklet each Lent, encouraging its use in the church throughout the country. Many of the SCCs use the booklet. The same material appears in the booklet in both Swahili and English.

The five topics treated in the 2001 Lenten booklet are: (1) Sacredness of the Environment, (2) Sacredness of the Economy, (3) Sacredness of Persons and HIV/AIDS, (4) The Constitution, and (5) Dignity of the Girl-Child. The presentation for each of the five is structured on the "see, judge, act" paradigm. A text presents the problem, and a full-page drawing illustrates each issue.

Picture the gathering around the topic "The Dignity of the Girl-Child." The house is very small and basic. There are eighteen people in the tiny living room, some standing or leaning against the wall because there are not enough chairs. Thirteen are women, five are men. One of the women has prepared the topic.

Here is the "see" situation, the illustration (opposite). John (eleven) and Maria (nine and a half) are in the same grade because John had to repeat a year. John is at the table doing homework. The father is reading the newspaper. The mother is in the kitchen preparing a meal, with a small child strapped across her bosom. She calls to Maria, "Maria, when you're through cooking, come and help me with the baby or the utensils." John intervenes, "But, Mummy, Maria hasn't done her homework yet. It's already late, and she won't be able to finish. The teacher won't be happy with her." Then the father says, "Oh, the teacher won't mind. She's only a girl."

One of the women in the house church presents the case for discussion. Almost immediately one of the men says that it's more important for a boy to have school because he will be the head of the house. This would be a common cultural presumption, and other

men nod in agreement. One of the men says that Paul tells Christians
that the man is the head of the household. So he has to be educated
to do that well. There is uneasy movement among the women, whose
facial expressions seem to say, "Something's just not right about this."

Then another woman recalls that Paul also says that, for those
who are baptized in Jesus Christ, distinctions and special treatment
aren't allowed for ethic origins, social class, or even gender. The
women relax a little. But now there's a new problem: Paul seems to be
saying two different things. A third woman speaks (she is a catechist in
the parish): "When I think I am hearing conflicting things in scripture, I go this way. Over and over the Bible says God wants all of his

children to be free from bondage. So if two passages seem to say opposite things, I say, 'which frees from bondage?'" With this guideline, which elicits a lot of positive nods, there seems to be agreement that gender should not decide where and how education is available and supported.

The woman asks, "If I have a son and a daughter, and only enough money for one to get a good education, how do I decide?" Another of the men, who hadn't spoken before, says, "The boy child, of course, because of the roles he has to play." Now these are not thoughtless, macho men. They are there willingly, and they stay with the discussion. But the way their culture thinks about gender roles is rooted deeply inside them, which non-men (women!) can see more easily. One of the women, who has been a frequent participant in the dialogue, says that her parents wanted to give further education to her brother, but he didn't want it, and it was not made available to her. She speaks of her hurt and continuing sadness because she loves to learn. One of the men and two of the women acknowledge her leadership gifts and her ability to express things clearly, which they don't have, and they say they are sad with her. This turns the conversation around still again. After more exchange, there is a consensus that if there is a financial limit on how much education is available to a child, preference should be given to the child with the best grades and the desire for it, whether boy or girl.

Here you have only the highlights of a conversation that lasted nearly three hours interspersed with a few breaks and refreshments. There was very moving give-and-take about experiences, ideas, feelings, and vested interests, and there was strong dialogue between faith and culture, although those words would not have been in the participants' minds or on their lips. There were substantial changes in how certain group members viewed the world, and there will perhaps be changed behaviors if the SCC keeps supporting the conclusions. It is no exaggeration to say that there was some conversion experience.

The best homilist in the world could not have facilitated the conversation between scripture and lived experience that occurred at this meeting. The dynamics of that kind of conversation promote ownership of the outcome. People participated in the process of shared experience.

The Reign/Kingdom of God

In a metaphor that resonated with the time of monarchies, God was the sole King/ruler of the people. He had intentions for how those people should be related to him, to each other, and to the rest of the world. When the people of God responded to God's intentions and collaborated with God in their realization, their historical experience was redeemed. For most people today, the experience of a reigning king is alien. And yet, while the kingship metaphor may be a stretch for people living in modern democracies, the basic notion still carries meaning for people rooted in a biblical faith: God has intentions for us that are salvific when realized.

In the prophet Micah, the Lord brings his people to trial for their failure to carry out his intentions for them. The Lord invites the people to try to defend themselves before the mountains, the hills, the foundations of the earth (Mic 6:1–2). And then, in a summary as brief and brilliant as anywhere in the Hebrew scriptures, God's intentions are rendered utterly clear to his people:

> He has told you, O mortal, what is good;
>> and what does the LORD require of you
> but to do justice, and to love kindness,
>> and to walk humbly with your God? (Mic 6:8)

Justice and mercy are the two characteristics of the Lord named regularly in the Hebrew scriptures, and when the world is holy the way God is holy—this being God's intention for us—then we live from justice *(tsedeq)* and mercy *(hesed)*. To walk humbly with God is a recognition of God's kingship and our vassalhood, or better for today, of God's redemptive love for the world and our reception of and collaboration with his care.

The reign of God is also Jesus' way of naming God's intentions for the world. There are seventeen references to the kingdom in Mark, thirty-seven in Luke, and forty-seven in Matthew. In John there are only five such references because John makes our attachment to Jesus the equivalent of God's will for us. While the use of "I" in deliberate self-reference occurs only nine times in Mark, ten in Luke, and seventeen in Matthew, it occurs 118 times in the fourth gospel. Whichever way we do the interpretation, the Reign of God has got to be our preoccupation and our occupation.

The gospel call is both radically personal and radically interpersonal, not as disparate strands but as the warp and woof of a single fabric. While the gospels remember the personal call from Jesus to follow him, saying "yes" always meant joining a group of followers. The Reign of God is equally social from God's perspective. The New Covenant is a covenant with a people. Kings did not make covenants with members of tribes one by one, but with a people as a social group, and all members of the social group were bound by the covenant by dint of belonging to the group. In Luke's Gospel, Jesus begins his public life in the synagogue by reading from Isaiah a passage concerning the promised reign of God. Jesus is the anointed one who brings good news to the afflicted, liberty to captives, sight to the blind, freedom to the oppressed. Already earlier in Luke, Mary proclaims, because of the child within her, that power arrangements will be upended and resources will be redistributed. And with a theologically social voice, the church teaches in the Second Vatican Council that it has pleased God to save us not one by one but as people mutually related (§9).

To put it differently, to be church fully is to be a community in permanent mission. The mission is two-fold. The *inner mission* is to the well-being of the members of our own community. The *public mission* is to the well-being of the social institutions and the culture in which we live. The notion of common good binds these two together. It is Jeremiah who articulates this connection with stunning clarity in the period of the Babylonian captivity. Writing from Jerusalem to the Jews in Babylon he records the Lord as saying, "But seek the welfare of the city where I have sent you into exile, and pray to the LORD on its behalf, for in its welfare you will find your welfare" (Jer 29:7). Biblical faith always has a public dimension, to which we are less accustomed to attend instinctively. The inner and public life should never subsume each other but neither should they be disconnected. We are the kind of people whose mission requires our togetherness, and whose togetherness demands that we be in mission. Gathering in SCCs sends us with the kind of sending that calls us back together.

To put it very simply, I cannot love someone deeply without caring about all those things about which that person cares. I feel the world with that person's feelings. Feeling the feelings of another is the very nature of sympathy, which Abraham Heschel says is the driving force in the heart of the prophet. In a small church community, the scriptures are privileged access to how God feels the world. The members' experience of the world, personally accessed through situational analyses, is clothed with God's feelings for the world. Because social analysis is a way of learning, as accurately as possible, the world that God feels with justice and mercy, social analysis doesn't just happen before or after prayer but can indeed be itself truly integral to the prayer act.

What Lies Ahead

Chapter 2, "The Wider Context," is a framing chapter. Here we name factors that contextualize small church communities. Some are church related, others reflect the larger culture. We will give an initial account of a small Christian community and the growth of SCCs during the recent dozen years. We have also named characteristics of American society and Catholic culture that are particularly relevant to the life of SCCs.

Because SCCs are a relatively new phenomenon, albeit with some features of the church of the first centuries, it is important to pay attention to their "churchhood." And that is the focus of Chapter 3. We want to engage ecclesiology, but also to use "extrarational" assistance from images and models because new work of the Spirit elicits poetry as well as logic.

Chapter 4 expresses our conviction, rooted in both theology and sociology, that a community is both gathered and sent. As gathered, it attends to the conversation of its inner life. As sent, it carries on a conversation with the larger world beyond its immediate constituency. We offer an understanding or practical theology as a privileged mode of conversation in the small Christian community. Practical theology gives configuration to both its inner and public life and also affirms the essential inner connection between them. SCCs are privileged locations where theology happens in place, near the action, with the benefit of participant wisdom.

Chapter 5 addresses many issues in a community's inner life and offers abundant practical, pastoral suggestions. We will address the issue of leadership, which the research suggested deserves focused pastoral formation. We think of the many ways in which Paul reminded the early communities how people who were members of each other were expected to comport themselves with each other. There is a behavioral logic in being the body of Christ.

Chapter 6 is about the public life of SCCs. It takes its theme, the shalom of the city, from Jeremiah 29. Even in the terrible circumstance of living in a city of exile, the prophet requires God's faithful to work for the good of that city and to pray to God for it, since people cannot find individual salvation (shalom) apart from the salvation of the city.

Chapter 7 is the closing witness of the authors of this book to the preciousness of community, to our valuation of SCCs as an adventure in the community called church, and consequently, to the kind of formation that this great experiment deserves, for the sake of the Kingdom.

2

The Wider Context:
American Society and Church Culture

Introduction

This is a lengthy chapter, speaking to three areas of concern: small Christian communities, their U.S. cultural environment, and their U.S. ecclesial environment.

In Part I of this chapter we indicate what we mean by "small Christian community," even though more detail gets filled in throughout the book. We also want to name and document the growth in SCC activities over the past dozen years. It has been formidable.

In Parts II and III we sketch the situation in broad strokes. We are not implying that most small communities self-consciously interact with all of the context we name, and we acknowledge that our description of context is both partial and selective. But these are major contexts that environ SCCs in the U.S. culture and in the U.S. Catholic Church. They provide us with insight into the world as it is, and into the world as it could be. How the world is now shapes SCCs, and how the world *might be* is possible mission for SCCs.

In Part II we are looking at American society from three perspectives: individualism, economics, and racism.

We examine the "individualism" that sociologists have long named as a fierce component of our cultural identity. Individualism simultaneously makes us wary of the commitments needed to form community and also makes us hunger for community; we need it so and yet avoid it so.

We then focus upon the economic system that prevails in this nation (and in much of the world beyond). It tends relentlessly to

move resources out of the fiscal bottom and middle and into the fiscal top, from which not much at all trickles down (as political rheto-
ric would try to have it). Robert Reich, in fact, speaks about the
secession of the successful, "the top 20% that is quietly seceding
from the rest of the nation" (Reich, 1991, 42). Their largesse "does
not flow mainly to social services for the poor…[but] to the places
and institutions that entertain, inspire, cure, or educate wealthy
Americans" (ibid). While the reign of God is certainly not dependent upon an economic system's functioning with justice, neither
does it get very far without it. Justice is the equitable distribution of
power as well as of goods, that is, the power to participate in decision-
making that affects our lives. Coalitions between the bottom and middle could have immense transformative power in respect to economic
justice and might well be a task for SCCs to confront explicitly.

    We also name racism as a cultural presence in the U.S., espe-
cially since its virulence is once more becoming visible. Because the
two of us are closest to relationships between African-American and
white communities in New Orleans, that will be our focus. (It could
just as well be between Anglos and Hispanics in another setting, and
so forth.) SCCs are not easily racially or socially mixed, which leaves
them in danger of being just gatherings of the like-minded, what
Robert Bellah calls lifestyle enclaves. But when SCCs are involved in
a broad-based community organization, interracial partnerships may
be achieved, though not easily.

    In Part III of this chapter we will address the Catholic eccle-
sial environment as context for the post-Conciliar emergence of
small Christian communities. One of the most obvious features is
the conflicted state of affairs in our church today. No anthropologist or sociologist would be surprised at so much conflict during a
period of fundamental systemic change; knowing it, however, does
not ease the pain of it. Our way of naming some of the deeper
impulses of our conflicted church will be with the metaphor of a
church that has two different birth certificates.

    A birth certificate is an accounting of one's origins. Each birth
certificate validates power arrangements that differ in both the location of power and in the way power functions. Power is certainly
among the most neuralgic issues in the contemporary Catholic
church. We will be naming that as a feature of contemporary ecclesial environment.

We will then speak to pluralism, which we are learning is a normative situation, not just a temporary condition on the way to shared agreement. Finding ways to affirm both normative pluralism and the possibility of a genuine community that embraces it is an ecclesial vocation to which small Christian communities might offer wisdom. While grappling with pluralism is never easy, it is more manageable in smaller systems like SCCs, than in huge, expansive institutional structures like the larger church. Our hope is that small church might experiment in behalf of large church, and that a "transfer of learning" might become viable.

We conclude Part III with a look at people's religious hungers, especially in the context of Catholic life. We are sacramental people: bread and wine, water and oil, movement and song, lights and aromas, beauty and devotion, Mary and so much more. These things matter to our relationships with God, with the things of the world, with ourselves, and with one another. Ritual has traditionally meant a lot to Catholics.

And yet church attendance is way down for Catholics; a recent study has regular church attendance at about 27 percent. It seems fair to conclude that institutional church life, overall, is not attending well to the nature of these religious hungers in their contemporary context—above all in respect to youth and young adults.

Insofar as membership in small Christian communities requires additional time and energy on the part of members, we believe we can presume that these are religiously motivated people in search of more than they are getting in traditional expressions of Catholic life. So we also pay attention to what is happening in Catholic piety and to what seems to be the religious attraction of SCCs.

Part I: The Nature of SCCs and Their Recent Sudden Growth

The Small Christian Community

Rev. Joseph Healy has collected over a thousand names and expressions for what we are calling "the small Christian community" in this book. The fact that it has so many names indicates a richness of experience that is not easy to pin down. When we were writing *Dangerous Memories* almost twenty years ago, it wasn't clear what terminology we should use to describe these groups in our country. Language about them was (and is) still developing. Some preferred "intentional Christian communities" (ICCs), which we tended to use in *Dangerous Memories*. Others used "basic Christian communities" (BCCs) after the Latin American phenomenon, or similarly, "basic ecclesial communities" (BECs). Some communities use the language of the early church, "house churches" (HCs). While the language remains fluid, there is a growing tendency in our American context to speak about "small Christian communities" (SCCs). We will, therefore, use that language often, but not exclusively.

The Institute for Ministry at Loyola in New Orleans completed a detailed empirical and theological study of SCCs funded by the Lilly Endowment. It has been published under the title *The Catholic Experience of Small Christian Communities* (Paulist Press, 2000). Here is an SCC profile based on that research:

1. Most SCCs have between six and twelve adult members. There are more women members than men. Some SCCs include children because families are members.

2. Most SCCs meet bi-weekly or weekly, some less frequently.

3. Leadership is nearly always lay leadership, and it tends to function in very collaborative, participative ways.

4. The majority of SCCs have a parish connection, most often as a result of the impact of the parish Renew program, or from the model of "Restructuring Parishes into Communities" used in parishes throughout the U.S. Some grassroots SCCs are not parish-connected in any formal way, even though they function more or less within the parish, and members attend Eucharist and parish activities. They were established on their own, not by parish initiatives and members want more community and/or mission than is offered by parish life.

5. There are several kinds of SCCs that have no parish connection at all. There are groups that call themselves intentional eucharistic communities. They regularly have Sunday Eucharist, either because they have ordained members among them, or because they make contacts with priests who will celebrate Eucharist for them.

Other communities find their inspiration in the charism of religious orders, like the Jesuit Christian Life Communities and the Lay Marianist Community network. This is a growing group. The most marginal of the communities are composed of people who are disaffected with or have been wounded by the institutional church but refuse to stop "being church," albeit doing it differently. The voice of their sanctified anger is as important as it is painful and difficult to hear.

A Decade of Sudden and Great Growth

Our book *Dangerous Memories* was written in 1984–85 and published in 1986. We were members of a small Christian community in Minnesota and knew that there were others around the country. Articles were beginning to appear. The movement was served by the *National Catholic Reporter*'s periodical *Gathering*, although that publication was discontinued after a few years. The basic Christian community movement in Latin America was becoming increasingly familiar.

The amount of new activity in the years since then is really quite amazing. Thousands of SCCs have emerged in the Catholic context alone, along with several national organizations and many diocesan offices to support them. Practically none of the organizations, activities, and resources to be described here even existed twenty years ago.

In 1986, a few people interested in small Christian communities met in Buena Vista, Colorado, to ponder the kind of network that would be useful to SCCs. Mike and Barbara Howard from Arvada, Colorado, were prime movers. The organization, also called Buena Vista, now holds an annual convention that draws several hundred people. It publishes a newsletter, *Buena Vista Ink*, that reports on community experiences at home and abroad, evaluates resources, and communicates news about events.

The North American Forum for Small Christian Communities was organized largely as a network for diocesan personnel with special responsibilities to assist SCCs. A subsequent interest, promoted by the late Rev. James Dunning, is the catechumenal possibilities for parish SCCs with regard to the Rite of Christian Initiation for Adults. Instead of forming an RCIA team to journey

with catechumens during the initiation rites and disbanding after-
wards, catechumens could be apprenticed to already existing communities with which membership could continue after initiation.
This idea is new, full of promise, and profoundly consistent with the
dynamics of RCIA.

The model program "Restructuring Parishes into Communities"
began with Fr. Art Baranowski, a priest of the Detroit Archdiocese
who took his own successful experience doing this on the road, giving
workshops in many dioceses throughout the United States. He makes
clear that he does not mean for small communities to be another program that a parish makes available, but rather they are a new way of
being parish. He works only with parishes in which the pastor and staff
are on board with the project. The National Alliance of Parishes
Restructuring into Communities nurtures this parish development.

The Renew program, which originated in Newark, New
Jersey, with the support of Archbishop Gerety and the program
development of Msgr. Thomas Kleissler, has been a remarkable
stimulus to the formation of SCCs, though that was not the original intent. Often, when the formal program had been completed,
group members had found the experience so positive and so much
personal bonding had occurred that they opted to continue gathering. Since then a Post-Renew program has been developed with
video and print material to encourage and nurture SCCs.

When the office that supported SCCs in the Seattle Archdiocese
was closed, a group of lay women and men initiated the Ministry
Center for Catholic Community to provide workshops and resources
for SCCs. Their booklets on the Church's social teaching, on special
topics, and on the seasons of Lent and Advent have been marketed
nationally. The Center has a mailing list of several thousand.

The Pastoral Office for Small Christian Communities in
Hartford, Connecticut, is a model for what can be achieved in a diocese. The Director, Bro. Robert Moriarty, S.M., is also a scripture
scholar. He oversees the publication of *Quest*, a seasonally published
lectionary-based program for SCCs. Originally prepared for the
local church, these materials are now used widely across the nation
(each printing is about 15,000).

The Sisters of St. Joseph in Minneapolis, St. Paul, publish a
lectionary-based guide for SCCs, *Sunday by Sunday*, edited by Sr.
Joan Mitchell. Like *Quest*, it is a widely used resource.

An office for Latin American/North American Church Concerns (LANACC) was initiated and is directed by Rev. Robert Pelton, C.S.C., at the University of Notre Dame. This important project keeps the two Americas in touch with each other's experience and reaches out as well to the larger scene with international convocations.

Sr. Rosemarie Jasinski of the Bon Secours community in Marriottsville, Maryland, organized a network of religious communities making concerted efforts at forms of associate membership. The network includes SCCs that live out of the power of a religious life charism, some of which are self-consciously engaged in a specifically lay appropriation of that charism. A regular newsletter has very recently been initiated.

SCCs among Hispanics in the U.S. Catholic Church have less formal structure and connections, and so are less easy to track in research. Culturally, however, Hispanics are much more open to community and commitment than are middle-class Anglos. There are 500–600 Hispanic SCCs, for example, just in the Rio Grande Valley in South Texas, especially in the Brownsville diocese. Hispanic Pastoral Planning at the national level has placed a high priority upon the small Christian community, and a Bishops' Pastoral has recently been issued to give guidance to the continuing development of small church communities, which is the bishops' preferred term. Sr. Ninfa Garza has been a key pastoral agent in the development of these communities.

The Loyola Institute for Ministry in New Orleans offers a master's degree in Pastoral Studies that has "Basic Christian Community Formation" as one of the possible specializations. Special courses in leadership and other dimensions of SCC life are offered in Loyola University's Institute for Pastoral Studies in Chicago. A number of other Catholic university programs also offer pastoral courses relevant to the life of SCCs.

In this list of activities relevant to SCCs, not one single item was in place during the 1984–85 year when we undertook the writing of *Dangerous Memories*. (Renew was active, but Post-Renew hadn't been invented.) While the phenomenon is young in this country, what has been documented above is an incredible and rather sudden evolution for such a short span of life!

This book continues the analysis we began in *Dangerous Memories* because so much has happened in the U.S. Catholic

Church in the intervening decade. We still hold strongly to our intuitive thoughts described on the opening page of *Dangerous Memories:*

> Earthquakes reshape the foundations of the world upon which our human constructions rest. They are part of the shifts the earth must make to keep its energies and counter-energies in balance. Something of earthquake potential has been rumbling through the Roman Catholic World for a generation now. Some dangerous things are being remembered…. (Lee/Cowan, 1986)

Our collective memory of the house church as a normative form of Christian life in the early centuries is helping to fund new imagination. Such memories are experienced as "dangerous" because they call parts of the settled order into question. They feel dangerous to whatever part of the status quo is interrogated by a memory of how it was once different than it is now. The interrogation is carried on anyway, with an interest in a new future. Dangerous memories always remind us that something else might be the case.

At the end of this book, we offer names, addresses, and phone numbers for many of the organizations, networks, and resources that might prove helpful to small Christian communities in the U. S. Catholic Church.

Part II: The Context of American Society

Individualism and the Need for Its "Socialization"

In the November 1996 issue of the food magazine *Bon Appetit*, the Ad Council ran a full-page statement praising volunteerism in U.S. culture (193). In the ad, a close-up of a coffee cup shows the following text printed on it:

> In America, you are not required
> to offer food to the hungry.
> Or shelter to the homeless.
> There is no ordinance forcing

you to visit the lonely, or comfort
the infirm. Nowhere in the
Constitution does it say you have
to provide clothing for the poor.
In fact, one of the nicest things
about living here in America
is that you really don't have
to do anything for anybody.

Then in small print at the bottom of the page, there was praise
for Americans who volunteered to do the above things, even though
they were not obliged to. This is a remarkably clear (and for many
of us, painful) statement of American individualism: we are not connected in ways that oblige us; any connection is voluntary, no matter what the need. This same advertisement also appeared on public
television.

In his well-known essay on "Self-Reliance," Ralph Waldo
Emerson echoes the same sentiment:

Then, again, do not tell me, as a good man did today, of
my obligation to put all poor men in good situations. Are
they *my* poor? I tell thee, thou foolish philanthropist, that
I grudge the dollar, the dime, the cent, I give to such men
as do not belong to me and to whom I do not belong.
(Emerson, 1983, 262)

The message here is the same: we do not belong to each
other in any way that obligates us. We can, of course, choose to
become connected, either because we like each other or because it
is useful.

In the 1830s an astute visitor to the U.S. from France, Alexis
de Tocqueville, described a kind of individualism in our national
culture that ran the risk of incarcerating people within themselves.
A series of sociological analyses of U.S. culture in recent decades
has continued that critique (Riesman, 1950; Sennet, 1960; Slater,
1970; Bellah, 1985). In *Habits of the Heart*, Robert Bellah and his
colleagues said that the very individualism that tends to close us
within ourselves also has the effect of creating a loneliness within us
as a cultural characteristic. Our individualism makes us hanker for

community, but it also stands in the way of the kind of commitment that community requires.

Habits of the Heart recommends that we look for usable historical memories in order to retain the goodness we have culled from our experiment with individualism, while redeeming that tradition from its excesses. Bellah names two memories that have been part of U.S. life: the small religious communities (biblical communities he calls them) and republican approaches to social issues, in the root sense of *res publica*, or concern for public issues. Republican instincts ask that people address public issues as close as possible to where the issues exist.

Robert Wuthnow's research, published as *Sharing the Journey* (1994), documents the upsurge in interest in support groups, to which 40 percent of Americans now belong. While he seems to feel that this is positive for U.S. culture, he names two reservations. Because the emphasis on mutual support is so strong, such groups often avoid tough issues, even among themselves. The penchant for smooth relations often domesticates groups, and when they then invoke God, they tend to domesticate God as well. Also, these groups tend to be preoccupied with their own internal issues, and relatively few of the groups he researched have a constitutive concern for issues beyond their own confines.

Small Christian communities in any location need to be in conversation with their culture from the perspective of their faith. Individualism is a critical context for SCCs in U.S. culture. We believe that theological reflection is a privileged mode of SCC conversation, which we will be addressing later under practical theology. This reflection can help us with a two-fold religio-cultural task: to preserve what we have learned from the U.S. experiment about the dignity of each individual life and to resocialize our interpretation of the individual as connected not by mere option but by obligation to the common good.

The hunger for community is real and well documented. But groups can also take on the individualistic characteristics of the lone person. SCCs stand a chance of participating in the resocialization of individuality without losing its beauty. As our book unfolds, that is part of the context for the importance of mutuality in our inner life and concern for the commonweal in our public life. The SCC has an important redemption to mediate, not alone, but as one place of grace in American religion.

Paul was a genius in knowing how to seize a moment. He stood upon the Areopagus, a great mound of rock just outside the entrance to the temple complex on the Acropolis in Athens. "Your genuine religious aspirations," he told the assembled crowd, "are expressed in your devotion to the unknown god. I know you care. I am here to tell you that I know that god's identity. Let me introduce you to God." And for a lot of those gathered there, Paul's strategy worked.

Those who understand the full power of the small Christian community are positioned to enter the marketplace of American society and say, "Your genuine hunger for community is expressed in the fact that one out of four of you now belongs to a support group. But there are groups and groups. Let us tell you about one called 'the body of Christ,' that both gathers people in and sends people out, and the world is better for it." This is truly good news.

Economics and Commonwealth

We who write this book live in a city where hope is hard to come by. There are too many homeless street people and empty houses in New Orleans. Public education is in crisis. Poverty is deep and haunts the lives of African Americans more than any other group. The murder rate is high, the largest percentage being black-on-black killing in areas where drug traffic thrives. Violence is so omnipresent that most people think twice before walking just about anywhere after dark and usually don't if they can help it. Our house in middle-class New Orleans has been broken into, and we have been mugged in our own driveway. This city, sadly, is not an isolated phenomenon in the United States. This is becoming the familiar narrative of urban sites.

Driving the violence is a widespread and deepening poverty. In an article in *America* (June 17, 1996), William Quigley reports upon the most recent data (1994) from the U.S. Census Bureau. The share of the nation's income that went to the top 20 percent of households rose to 46.7 percent, an average annual income of $105,945. The bottom 20 percent averaged an annual income of $7,762.

"Net worth" is another kind of gauge. This figure includes property, cars, investments, and bank accounts—all of this minus outstanding debts. The 1994 data follows:

	Percentage of Nation's Wealth	Average of Net Worth
Lowest 20%	–00.64	–$ 7,075 [debt]
Next Lowest 20%	+01.58	+ $ 17,503
Middle 20%	+05.56	+ $ 61,777
Next Highest 20%	+12.77	+ $ 141,778
Top 20%	+78.47	+ $ 871,463

This is not just a recent phenomenon. Over a two-century period of U.S. history, resources have steadily been relocated out of the bottom and the middle into the upper 20 percent (Osberg, 1984, 44):

	1776 % Distribution of Nation's Wealth	Two Centuries Later
Lowest 30%	2%	0%
Middle 50%	30%	15.4%
Top 20%	68%	84.6%

An old proverb says, "War is too important to be left to the generals." So while we are not economists, we try to be decently informed citizens. We feel confident in our grasp of a biblical guideline. As simplistic as it may seem, a biblical understanding of creation and the human community holds that the earth is the shared home of all of God's creatures and that all of God's people have a right to the necessities of life. Once everyone has enough, anyone can have more than enough. All people also have the right to a voice in decisions that impact upon them. We agree with the critique of John Paul II that thus far no version of either socialism or capitalism has measured up to these biblical guidelines. Whether another economic system is needed, whether one of the two named systems can be revised to serve the commonweal, or whether a combination could succeed, we do not pretend to know.

The first question that people must address is what kind of life they should build for themselves and their children, what they want human community to look like. This is the commonweal. Human community/society is the overarching system. All of our other systems are ancillary to the good of the community.

We will state the issue a little more theoretically. We are giving centrality to the question, what do we want our world to look like? For Christians, the same question is about God's intentions for our world and our collaboration with God's intentions. All of the subsystems in our lives should serve the needs of the human community. Economics is one such subsystem. Economics, however, has been emerging as the overarching system rather than a sub-system. As such, it asks what kind of community serves its purposes best (NAFTA is an example). In their respective books indicated below, Robert Simons and Barry Schwarz address this central question about human nature and the social systems at our disposal. Robert Simons proposes "the radical need to move from viewing social relationships as embedded in an existing economy, to holding economic systems accountable to already existing sets of human relationships and communities" (Simons, 1995, x).

We confess that addressing the above situation in any way that stands a chance of altering the system is daunting. The gap between rich and poor is larger in the United States than in any of the other dozen and a half industrial countries in the world. The aggregate control of the economy by multinational corporations does not seem susceptible to much external influence. So why raise this as a context for the life of small Christian communities? Partly, at least, because our voice, however small, is still a voice. This was certainly an operative conviction at the Fourth Congress of European Base Communities, held in Paris in 1991. The agenda for the Congress was formulated through consultation with base communities in many countries of Europe. Economics was at the top of agenda items. Profound concern for the impact of an emerging European Economic Community was named again and again at the Paris meeting.

In this country, as we have indicated above, the same basic dynamics that drive the economy are responsible for worsening the overall situation of both the middle class and the very poor (certain dynamics make it better, of course, but that is not the fundamental narrative structure). We believe in the possibility of effective alliances and coalitions between the poor and the middle, and in their potential as a Catholic voice and motivator of the larger church, and would like to address this possibility.

The Middle and the Poor: Alliances and Coalitions

One of the large differences between Latin American base communities and U.S. small Christian communities is that the large majority of base community members are very poor. In most Latin American countries, in fact, there is no sizeable middle class comparable to that of the United States and Canada. In Latin America, therefore, the power for social change resides largely among the poor once they are conscientized and organized. Some of the important leadership for conscientization and organization in basic ecclesial communities has come from the church, from sisters, brothers, priests, theologians, and sometimes bishops as well. But parts of the church, both locally and in Rome, have also resisted the development of base communities. In many Latin American countries (notably Brazil), base communities have been responsible for significant social programs and social changes that benefit the poor. But members have also been persecuted by military and police and have lost their lives.

In the U.S. the majority of small Christian communities are middle class, although the minority of Hispanic communities is not small, and most of them are among the poor and working class. If middle-class membership differentiates U.S. communities from Latin American communities, there is also an essential similarity, for there is immense power for social action and social change in the middle class in the U.S. The role of middle-class leadership and middle-class activity has been demonstrably present in the peace movement, civil rights movement, lettuce boycotts in support of the Farm Workers' movement, boycotts of both Nestle and Campbell soup products because of policies, the Green Peace movement and so on. Probably no single group has been as effective in leading the U.S. Catholic Church into a post-Conciliar age than women religious, whose membership is mostly middle class.

We are convinced that if the middle class and the poor form effective alliances and coalitions, their prophetic voice and prophetic action can matter a great deal more. What underlies that persuasion is our conviction that the middle class is being steadily disempowered, that poverty is deepening, and that the causes of both phenomena are fundamentally the same economic policies.

The following analyses depend upon a cluster of studies, and what is pictured is painted from their reflections as well as from our own experience. We want to name these helpful resources here and recommend them as part of the exercise of practical theology in SCCs, to be discussed at length in Chapter 4: *Commonwealth: A Return to Citizen Politics* by Harry Boyt; *Economic Justice for All* by the Catholic Bishops of the U.S.; *The Want Makers* by Eric Clark; *The Imperial Middle* by Benjamin DeMott; *A Journey Through Economic Time* by J. Kenneth Galbraith; *Who Will Tell the People* by William Greider; *The Holy Use of Money* by John Haughey; *Claims in Conflict: Retrieving and Renewing the Catholic Human Rights Tradition* by David Hollenbeck; *Risking Liberation: Middle Class Powerlessness and Social Heroism* by Paul King, Kent Maynard, and David Woodyard; *Still Following Christ in a Consumer Society* by John Kavanaugh; *Economics for Prophets* by Walter Owensby; *The Politics of Rich and Poor* and *The Boiling Point* by Kevin Phillips; the book *The Work of Nations* and *The New York Times Magazine* article "The Secession of the Successful" by Robert Reich; and *The Battle for Human Nature: Science, Morality and Modern Life* by Barry Schwartz.

"Middle class" is a cultural classifier. When both of us were children, our families lived on the income of one person (the father). Our parents bought a modest house, owned a used car, and paid tuition for their children in Catholic schools. Our parents worked hard to become respectable, self-made people who were better off than their parents and whose children would be better educated and more affluent than they were. They had a small amount of surplus. They felt relatively secure about being in charge of their lives. They could count on retirement and social security and did not worry terribly about the future. Those days are over!

While it may not have been all that easy, the 1950s middle-class family lived on one income from 40 hours a week of work. Today it takes double that amount of income so that two wage earners are the case for most middle-class families today. When both parents must work, family life is altered in radical ways. There is a decreasing sense of economic security. Middle-class people often feel relatively little control of their work space or their political reality. Health care and education costs have soared so quickly that middle-class people are chronically nervous about the future. They no longer presume that their children will be better educated, more affluent, and more secure than themselves. The middle class is led to believe that welfare programs are responsible for their plight; in fact, the shift in tax burdens is a far larger cause. Between 1977 and 1989 the effective federal tax rates for the lowest 20 percent of families in this country increased .1 percent and for the next 20 percent increased 1.4 percent. At the same time for the top 20 percent of families the tax burden dropped 5.8 percent, with a 13.5 percent decrease for the top 5 percent, and a 24.7 percent rate decrease for the top 1 percent of families (Phillips, 1993, 282).

Three characteristics of today's middle class are that they tend to be patriotic, to be religious, and to behave in consumerist ways. Pecuniary envy, the incessant desire to have more money, drives consumerism. Advertising invites all Americans to dream upwards, but the spending that middle-class Americans presume will get them there has in effect impoverished them and burdened them with "things" rarely used. How often do most middle-class families use a formal living room and dining room when they have a large family room and a sizable dining area adjoining the kitchen? But middle class dwellings are regularly built with that rarely used space.

Clark's book on advertising details how VALS, which stands for "Values and Life Styles," sizes us up. VALS, a typology for classifying potential consumers, was developed by social scientists at the SRI Research Center, Menlo Park, California (Clark, 1988, 163–71). VALS serves AT&T, Avon, Coca-Cola, General Motors, Proctor and Gamble, Reynolds, Tobacco, Tupperware, and so on. They have analyzed the spending propensities of nine categories of people gathered into four groupings:

Group A—Need Driven
    1. 4%—survivors (very poor and elderly)
    2. 7%—sustainers (edge of poverty, younger people)
Group B—Outer Directed (they respond quickly to signals about
           what they should do/have)
    3. 38%—belongers (they want to fit in, not eager to
      stand out)

4. 20%—achievers (competitive, eager to stand out)
5. 10%—emulators (upwardly mobile, very ambitious)
Group C—Inner Directed (try to live according to values)
  6. 3%—people on the move from outer to inner
    directed
  7. 5%—mature, willing to experiment
  8. 11%—socially conscious, very responsive to social
    need
Group D—Integration of both Inner and Outer Motivation
  9. 11%—balance of inner and outer, can be appealed to
    on both counts, self-determinative

When VALS worked with Timex to enter the health-care market (making, for example, digital thermometers and blood-pressure monitors), they targeted #4 (achievers) and #9 (socially conscious), and within a year three of Timex's products were top sellers nationally. We in the middle class are easy prey to advertising that first makes us want and then turns our wants into needs.

Even in the best of circumstances, it is very difficult to refuse to get caught up in the dynamics of a consumerist culture. What makes it easier for most of us in the middle class to take a stand is to have connected in a substantial personal way with the poor of the world. And yet we've learned through social analysis that our sacrifices (individually cutting back on consumerist behavior) will not change the system that disempowers both the bottom and the middle. Token sacrifices do not alter a system unless they are powerful enough to alter consciousness.

Those of us who work for the church know that the least attended classes, workshops, and lectures are those about social justice. Middle-class guilt is paralyzing. To break free of this guilt and to mobilize, we should take seriously what Abraham Heschel says about the basic message of the prophets, that while all are responsible, few are guilty. We believe that Yahweh would rather have all the people of God enjoy sufficiency. The elimination of middle-class sufficiency would not of itself create an equitable world. There is systemic dysfunction that worsens the plight of the bottom *and* the middle. Our recommendation for small Christian communities is that we find ways to form effective coalitions with those whose poverty and need are severe. We agree with the conclusion of

Risking Liberation, that individual efforts can do little, but that social heroism has potential. Connections between the bottom and the middle could be fertile ground for collective social heroism. Addressing critical, unmet human need is noble motivation. Knowing that coalitions between the middle and the poor stand a better chance of addressing the disempowerment of the middle as well is perhaps less altruistic, but not unnoble.

Long ago, in his book *Christ in a Pluralistic Age*, John Cobb reminded Christians that a Christological function of Jesus is to end poverty. We should not find Christ, therefore, simply "in the poor," but rather in our identification with everything in the poor that wants to stop being poor. We have already named the serious issue of when profit-driven market economics becomes the over-arching system served by other systems, rather than a subordinate system that serves the overarching common good. While it is important not to be naive about this nor about the possibility of significant transformation, we want to acknowledge not only for socio-economic reasons but for gospel reasons that coalitions which pressure systems are important expressions of faith's pub-lic life At the same time we also believe that profit motives can indeed be a moving force in a system that takes the common good seriously. We spend more time in chapter 6 on broad-based com-munity organizations because that has been our best experience of finding essential common ground between the poor and the middle.

Racism

We address the issue of racism from our own social location. We are white, and we live in New Orleans where the most palpable expressions of racism involve whites and African Americans. *Mutatis mutandis*, there are many versions of racism alive in our nation. In our social location our best-sustained experience in multiracial community has been in a broad-based community organization in which African American and white members of religious congrega-tions work together to build a more just world. The collaboration is not always easy. As white women and men, we are challenged to confront our own complicity in racism. We also want to ponder the redemptive potential of SCCs in this regard.

Division along racial lines is perhaps the most significant challenge to the survival, decency, and well-being of public life in the United States today. In urban America the unhealed wounds of racism lurk beneath the surface of ongoing conflicts about education, jobs, housing, and public safety. In national debate on public policy, the issues of affirmative action and immigration may stretch the nation's civility to its breaking point. In these circumstances, as our colleague Rev. Dwight Webster of Christian Unity Baptist Church insists, "color blindness" is just another name for blindness.

At this juncture in our history there is no prospect for a livable communal future unless explicit, honest, and respectful public conversations about race can be deliberately initiated and sustained within a web of lasting relationships grounded in shared action in the pursuit of mutual interests. The healing of racism and its associated devastations is imaginable only if we can engage one another in dialogue across the now-paralyzing boundaries of racial separation, endure the necessary tension of such engagements, and develop powerful interracial instrumentalities for acting in good faith to bring about the transformations of our common life such exchanges will demand of us. It's of limited value to talk about race if such talk is not wedded to the power to act collaboratively for the continuing transformation of racist institutions and attitudes.

We must work so that a seasoned and tested ability to cross racial lines and engage one another in direct conversation and in joint decision-making about our common life gradually becomes integral to the public culture of the United States. Such conversations must include the dangerous topics of race itself. Otherwise, the divisions among us, of which race is the most potent, will continue to cripple and may eventually destroy our capacity to strengthen the peace of our common life.

Action-oriented conversation across such barriers requires a context, a place in the real world within which it can happen. In our judgment the best instance of such a place today is found in broad-based community organizations like those affiliated with the Industrial Areas Foundation Network, which we will discuss in chapters 4 and 6. In these organizations citizens and people of faith join together through their congregations, schools, and civic associations, crossing lines of race, creed, and class. They work together both to develop a practical agenda for the well-being of their diverse

communities based on mutual interests and respect for differences
and to build a power base for making that agenda felt within the
arena of public decision-making. In more than sixty communities
throughout the United States, as well as in the United Kingdom and
South Africa, such organizations have been making a difference in
public education, law enforcement, job training, economic development, home ownership, medical care, and a variety of other critical
issues of public life for the past twenty-five years.

The significance of broad-based community organizations
rests not only on their formidable political astuteness and effectiveness, but on their potential as crucibles for the reconstruction of
civic culture in a pluralistic world. A crucible is a vessel which will
not melt when the ingredients it holds are heated to a point where
they are transformed. The conversation about race that will be
required if we are to be healed personally and collectively is one that
will generate serious heat, including rage, shame, and anxiety. It
needs a container that will not melt when such intense emotions
arise. By deliberately and patiently building and sustaining relationships across the usual barriers of race, creed, and class, relationships
characterized by authentic public conversation, broad-based community organizations may become those crucibles. Our ten-year
experience in one of these organizations—The Jeremiah Group in
New Orleans—leads us to conclude that it is in learning to act
together for the common good within such carefully cultivated public relationships that African Americans and whites have our best
opportunity to create the conditions required for reconciling the
devastating racist history that continues to burden us all.

Risking engagement in public conversation for the common
good across racial lines, including a critical examination of ideological "whiteness," is how we might heal the divisions of racism.
Sociologist Frank Wright once observed that "most of us perhaps
owe more to violence done on our behalf than we realize" (Wright,
1987, 269). Violence historically done to others in public life—in
the arena of politics, economics, and culture—must be publicly rec-
onciled. New promises must be made and kept in the pluralistic
public square of our time. Denying America's race problem means
allowing the redemptive possibility of a culturally diverse public life
to sink beneath the weight of slavery and racism. Through the vehicle of participation in broad-based interracial organizations, SCCs

now have the opportunity to participate in the creation of a truly inclusive public life in which no privilege is granted or withheld because of gender, race, or social class. The motivations for Christians could not be clearer: "For those baptized into Christ Jesus there can be neither Jew nor Greek, there can be neither slave nor freeperson, neither male nor female—for all of you are one in Christ Jesus" (Gal 3:26–28).

Part III: The Context of Ecclesial Culture

The Metaphor of "Birth Certificate"

In the contemporary culture of the Catholic Church there are other deep divides, deep enough to become a chasm if we do not come to terms with them. Cardinal Joseph Bernardin's plaintive cry for dialogue in the months before his death responded to the pain and dividedness we experience.

A useful way of looking at one of these divides is using the metaphor of "birth certificate" to reflect on how the church understands itself. Birth certificate stands for the church's interpretation of how it came to be. This is no minor matter: our memories of where we came from drive the anticipations out of which futures are created. Not only are there alternative futures, there are alternative pasts. Perhaps, more truly, there are alternative futures *because* there are alternative pasts.

Collective remembering adds more completeness to a community; but it is no less selective than individual memory. Collective remembering is fuller, but it may also be more unbalanced because it can concentrate the force of its selectivity and thus deepen *excluded* memory.

Nietzsche's well-known observation that there is no such thing as an uninterpreted fact applies to memory as well. Every memory is selective, and no one remembers anything perfectly and in its entirety. Our present situation is one of the factors that shapes selectivity. We are learning, for example, that poor people remember history differently than affluent people, that African Americans remember history differently than white Americans, that women remember history differently than men. People in every social location have vested interests in how a past gets remembered. By this we do not mean consciously manipulated memory, but rather, that our interests inevitability shape even unconscious retrievals.

Catholics have two memories about how we began as church, two birth certificates. We will call the first a Doctrinal Birth Certificate. The Doctrinal Birth Certificate has been long in the making. Augustine's sense of the church would be an example. There are seeds of it already in the later documents of the New Testament, like the pastoral letters to Timothy and Titus. In the defensive ecclesiology of the Counter-Reformation and in subsequent centuries until Vatican II, this doctrinal version of church origins has been the centerpiece of a Roman Catholic imagination about itself.

The second we will call a Biblical Birth Certificate, though more than scripture is included. While it feels like a much "newer" Birth Certificate, it is in fact an older one that has only been recently discovered and is even now still being unfolded. Critical biblical scholarship during the twentieth century has hugely reshaped our conversations with our early texts and our early history. Biblical hermeneutics (a theory of interpretation) has taught us both the intricacies of memory and the performative or transformative character of the texts we create. These new memories result in a very different perception of church origins.

Differing memories about where we came from create different understandings of who we are now and how our future narrative is to be written. That is why emotions run high around these issues: they are not just about a past, but about essential present identity and about the allocation of energies and resources for the church to whose upbuilding we are committed.

Doctrinal Birth Certificate

The church of the Doctrinal Birth Certificate was founded by Jesus in fidelity to his Father's intentions for him and for the world. Because most Jews do not elect to become followers of Jesus, this New Covenant replaces the Old Covenant, the sole purpose of which, according to the Doctrinal Birth Certificate, was to prepare the way for the new. The use of Old Testament texts in Matthew's Gospel, for example, makes this clear.

The Apostles provided the basic paradigm for the later development of the church. They were an Apostolic College which provided the nascent church community with the leadership that Jesus willed. The College of Bishops is the direct successor of the College of Apostles.

Peter was the pre-eminent Apostle to whom the leadership was entrusted in a special way. The popes are the successors to Peter. In earlier church history, the popes were called "Vicars of Peter." It is a later tradition in which they are called "Vicars of Christ." To safeguard the faith of the church, infallibility was conferred upon Peter in Matthew 16:18–19 and upon the College of Apostles in Matthew 18:16.

When the sacramental system of the Catholic Church was called into question during the Reformation, the Counter-Reformation's Council of Trent affirmed that there are seven sacraments, that this has always been the case, and that each sacrament was individually and specifically instituted by Jesus Christ. Theology, then, speculates on the moments of institution. Baptism and Eucharist are the easiest to document in the New Testament. The ordination of the Apostles as priests of the New Testament occurs at the Last Supper when Jesus charges them to "Do this in memory of me."

While throughout the centuries the church has elaborated its understanding of Christian life, the deposit of faith closed with the completion of the New Testament. The deposit of faith and the structures and teachings of Jesus are non-negotiable.

Since then, the Holy Spirit has continued to direct the church and to assure its faithfulness, especially in the guidance of the pope and the College of Bishops in their roles of governing, teaching, and sanctifying the faithful of Jesus Christ.

The existence of religious orders of men and women does not begin in New Testament times, nor even soon after. But they are founded in the evangelical counsels of celibacy, poverty, and obedience given the church by Jesus in his lifetime.

It is worth noting that ecclesiology, such a standard branch of Catholic theology today, did not become a specific discipline until after the Reformation, when the institutional aspect of the church was called into question in many areas. In the *Summa*, for example, Thomas Aquinas does not have a tract on church. He moved directly from Christology to the sacraments. Much of the Doctrinal

Birth Certificate's articulation, therefore, developed from the sixteenth century onward.

It is only in more recent times, especially beginning with Leo XIII, that the teaching of Jesus regarding social justice as belonging to the essential character of the Reign of God has become more explicit in the church. This is an essential and welcome retrieval.

Biblical Birth Certificate

"Biblical" is shorthand for the kind of biblical historical research that begins to show up already in the late 1700s with Hermann Samuel Reimaurus. He wrote an essay to the effect that the aims of Jesus and the aims of his disciples were not identical. This initiated over a century of biblical studies that attempted to use the same historical methods developing in secular history writing. At the beginning of the twentieth century, Albert Schweitzer's criticism of this quest for the historical Jesus helped redirect historical research, not only about scripture but also about the very early period of Christian history. These methods, refined over time, continued to meet resistance in Catholic thought until well after Vatican II, notwithstanding Pius XII's approval of historical methodology (form criticism) in scripture study.

Resistance is understandable. After all, the current historical and hermeneutical tools and methodologies were simply unavailable to the church's self-interpretation for most of its 1,900 years. But opposition to certain self-reinterpretations proposed by modern scholarship has been fierce. The regrettable modernist controversy in the late nineteenth and early twentieth centuries documents a stubborn ecclesial resistance to historicized self-interpretation.

The immense amount of historical research about the church and its origins has at last begun to impact upon the Doctrinal Birth Certificate. This influence is clear, for example, in the Second Vatican Council's document on liturgy and the restoration of the Rite of Christian Initiation for Adults. In addition, historical and biblical retrievals are responsible for the priority given to the people-of-God ecclesiology in *Lumen Gentium*. Also, one of the lesser-explored but far-reaching testimonies of Vatican II about Christian origins occurs in the church's affirmation in *Nostra Aetate* that "God does not repent of the gifts God made" to the Jews (foremost among them, covenant), that Jews remain "most dear to God," and that they have not been repudiated by God (§4).

We have barely begun to reflect on what is meant by "New Testament" once we affirm God's continuing covenant with the Jews. It appears very unlikely that Jesus' self-understanding included the founding of a new religious community outside of Judaism. The early communities, as Acts clearly reflects, honored Jewish history and holy places as well as their own eucharistic table community. *Nostra Aetate* makes it difficult for Catholics to interpret the "Jesus movement" as a termination of God's covenant (the "Old" Testament) with the Jews, and its replacement by a new one (the "New" Testament). It calls part of the legacy of the Doctrinal Birth Certificate into question and cries out for a permanent relationship between the synagogue and the church.

However, while the Biblical Birth Certificate requires critical reevaluation of parts of the Doctrinal Birth Certificate, it is not calling the church into question, but how the church accounts for itself and for the proactive presence of the Holy Spirit in its formation.

We offer a brief version ("birth certificate") of church origins that reflects the historical methodologies alluded to above. Probably no one scholar has described it exactly as we do, but the interpretations are all to be found in current respected scholarship.

Jesus initiated a reform movement with Judaism. He was a lay Jew who did not step out of Judaism to be who he was or do what he did. His repeated insistence in Matthew's Gospel that he came for the House of Israel is probably an accurate memory. At the close of Matthew's Gospel, Jesus tells the Apostles to baptize all nations in the name of the Father, of the Son, and of Holy Spirit. Most Matthean scholars agree that this ending was added to Matthew at a later time and reflects in its language the baptismal liturgy that had developed.

No follower of Jesus in the Christian scriptures was called a priest. That language for interpreting the role of the leader of Christian communities did not become prominent until the third century. In the Letter to the Hebrews Jesus is called our High Priest, but this is a metaphor. It discloses the Christological meaning of Jesus, but it does not disclose biographical information. Jesus was a lay Jew and not a priest. He was from the kingly family

(David), not the priestly family (Levi). And we know the name of the actual high priest during Jesus' time.

There is no textual indication that Jesus ordained anyone. As Raymond Brown long ago concluded, there was no need for a priesthood in Jesus' time because his followers were all within Judaism, which already had a functioning temple priesthood (Brown, 1970, 13–45).

The church structures familiar to us developed over time and were influenced by the structures of civil society. The Spirit has guided the church in its development, working through (not around) the normal ways of life within various cultures and ages.

Restoration/Refounding

It is commonplace today to distinguish between a restoration impulse and a refounding impulse. The two categories are a typology. Typologies reflect clear tendencies. However, their insights are only partial, and probably nothing is all one kind and none of the other.

These two approaches to change are not identical to the two birth certificates, but have similar impulses. The restorationist inclination tends to rely on the doctrinal birth certificate. It remembers a settled time when seminaries were full and religious orders thrived, when Mass was well attended and ritual was high and beautiful, when the sense of tradition was esteemed, and authority was rarely questioned by Catholics. This settled period accepted church order because what came directly from Jesus Christ is and must be "the way it is." This was not a begrudging acceptance, not a hesitant, questioning acceptance. The restorationist impulse wants as much of that back as we can reasonably reassemble within today's circumstances, because it was and is right. This is not a desire merely to repeat, but to retrieve what has been lost and to do it in ways that are faithful to the church's self-interpretation under a Doctrinal Birth Certificate.

The refounding impulse, because it tends to rely on the Biblical Birth Certificate, feels that its memory leaves it freer than does the Doctrinal Birth Certificate to imagine alternative futures. The danger of the refounding impulse is that it can become biblicist in ways that ignore church development under the Spirit. One can't just leap over 1,900 years of tradition. The strength of the refounding impulse is in a refusal to absolutize historically contingent forms of church; a Spirit at work in earlier institutionalizations of church can be a creative power in new institutional forms as well. But discerning the Spirit now, as discerning the Spirit then, is no simple matter.

The small Christian community has not been common since the early centuries, unless one counts communities of religious orders. It is true that community movements have sprung up in church history, such as those in response to Joachim of Fiore, but these have been very localized. In the last few decades, small Christian communities have become a phenomenon of all five continents, in a great variety of forms, and for many reasons. Even when embraced by the hierarchy, they were not simply its brainchild. They more easily claim a rationale for themselves from a Biblical than a Doctrinal Birth Certificate. However, because so many SCCs in this country are also parish connected, they are perhaps in a position where dialogue between the churches with the two birth certificates can fruitfully occur, less at the theoretical level of discourse, though that too, and more at the grassroots level of experience.

Pluralism and Dialogic Community

The two birth certificates and the contrasting restoration and refounding impulses are but two examples of the deepening pluralism within the Catholic church, a situation likely to remain normative. We should, therefore, address pluralism as a key contextual feature of Catholicism in this country. To be sure, pluralism is a church experience throughout the world; but we have our own particular appropriation of it within American Catholicism.

Announcing the Common Ground project in a press conference in August 1996, Cardinal Joseph Bernardin, Archbishop of Chicago, said,

> I have been troubled that an increasing polarization within the church and, at times, a mean-spiritedness have hindered the kind of dialogue that helps us address our mission as a church and our concerns as a church. As a result, the unity of the church is threatened...the faithful

members of the church are weary and our witness to government, society and culture is compromised.

He said these things in the context of a paper, "Called to be Catholic: Church in a Time of Peril," prepared by a group that included bishops, priests, religious women, and lay Catholics. The paper is an invitation to find forms of dialogue that allow us to confront differences in honest, direct dialogue.

Some people feel that genuinely honest discussion will eliminate differences and result in unanimity. And indeed, there are forms of difference which, if our conversation is good and our minds and hearts are open, we can transcend. But not all pluralism is subject to this resolution and it is here that we suggest a possible contribution from SCCs. Our focus is on a normative kind of pluralism and the need to learn new forms of community that are able to assimilate pluralism. Is community possible based not upon homogeneity but upon commitment to a respectful, even loving form of dialogue that keeps relationship among its diverse members intact?

Historical consciousness is the awareness of all the ways in which our experience, understanding, and articulations are conditioned by experience, history, language, education, temperament, and so on. There is no such thing as being unbiased. There is no uninterpreted fact. There is no way to transcend entirely all conditioning factors in order to arrive at "untarnished" objectivity. We are all biased, and we have to live with all of the ways in which our differences are embedded early on in our presuppositions and all of the ways in which these differences leave permanent reminders. This is what we mean by normative pluralism—the kind that does not go away; and that is the most serious kind with which church needs to come to terms. Assent to normative pluralism does not imply that all interpretations are equally valid or that we may not dispute them—only that we recognize each one's probable permanence and know that we must still remain together in human community or in church.

We applaud the effort to engage in serious respectful dialogue. But to expect to return to an earlier kind of consensus based upon a shared understanding of church teaching is not realistic. Besides that, we probably romanticize the unity we once had. Catholic thought has always had unruly propensities. The pressure today, however, arises peculiarly from our historical consciousness. In the preface of his book, *Plurality and Ambiguity*, David Tracy writes:

> What the "essence of Christianity" might be after Christians seriously acknowledge first, the plurality within their own traditions, second, the import of the many other religious traditions for Christian self-understanding and third, the profound cognitive, moral, and religious ambiguity of Christianity itself is, to put it mildly, a very difficult question. (1987, 10)

It will probably be easier in SCCs than in the larger institutional church to experiment with a form of community called "dialogic." When dialogic community succeeds, it is a stellar example of true conversation at work. For this form of community to work, members must make a few conversational commitments:

1. When I speak, I will do it in a way that gives you the best chance at understanding exactly what I hold and why I hold it. I am speaking so that you will understand me, not in order to convince you.
2. When I listen, my sole intention is to hear you in order to understand you. I will let your words mean what they mean to you, not what they perhaps mean to me. I will not listen in order to refute, but to understand.
3. I promise up front that I will not withdraw from the conversation, no matter how difficult it might become. I won't go away.
4. It will be okay for us to disagree, to argue, and to challenge—but not until our achievement of the first three points is accomplished.

This is not the way church has traditionally handled differences. Its habitual modes were developed during nineteen centuries before our self-understanding could be conditioned by historical consciousness. Even now we do not yet have widely disseminated skills in ecclesial culture for this kind of conversation, and accepting some kinds of pluralism as normative is a new experience. Skills in the dynamics of dialogic community are not likely to enter ecclesial culture from the top down. They probably have to be experimented with and developed at grassroots levels.

We are suggesting that SCCs are at least one place where we can explore whether dialogic community is a possible gift to the body (politic) of Christ. Small Christian communities are a place where the church can experiment with dialogic community as an ecclesial model; when SCCs do this, they *are* the experimenting church. New possibility rarely—perhaps never—appears first in a society's center. Possibility gets its first credentials in the margins.

Power

Words like *power* and *politics* badly need to be rehabilitated, as they are present in any human interaction. How power functions is a major issue in the contemporary church. In his letter *Ut Unum Sint*, Pope John Paul II recognized that even the exercise of papal power needs to be assessed (not whether, but how). It is our sense that SCCs are experimenting with models of power that are pertinent to the larger ecclesial body as well.

Jesus did not give his community of followers any specific structure for the function of power. Instead He offered root metaphors: how shepherds function (especially their penchant for the stray); how stewards function (they do not "own" the community but try to make it work well on someone else's behalf); and how servants function (they do not create the agenda, they serve it). Our reflections here refer particularly to the servant metaphor for how power functions.

Mark's Gospel recounts that when Jesus and the disciples were on the road, John and James approached Jesus and asked him for a special place above the others (Mark 10:35–44). When the others heard of this, they were miffed with John and James. Jesus took them all to task, saying that power must be understood very differently in the reign of God on earth. Leaders mustn't lord it over others, as pagans do, who want to make their authority felt. Rather, the leader is at the lower end of the traditional power structure, where the servant is found.

The disciples in Mark's Gospel were usually very slow to catch on. In Matthew's version of the same story, it was the mother of James and John, rather than those two themselves, who asked Jesus for privilege for her sons. The message was the same. Servanthood, not prestige or naked power, is the name of the game in Christian community.

In Luke's Gospel no names are mentioned (Luke 22:24–27), and we're told just that a dispute arose among them. It is stunning that Luke places this same scene at the Last Supper immediately after the treachery of Judas was foretold. We can only speculate why. Power issues must have often arisen in the Christian community for the instruction about servant leadership to be placed in such a precious setting. The text suggests that Jesus himself was serving them at table: "For who is greater, the one who is at the table or the one who serves? Is it not the one at the table? But I am among you as one who serves" (Luke 22:27).

That the issue has moved from discourse to drama is clear in John's Gospel (John 13:2–16). The scene once again is the Last Supper. Jesus removes his outer garment and dresses as a servant, towel around his waist, and washes his disciples' feet. "Now copy my example," he tells them. He whom the disciples rightly call "Master" and "Lord" does the dirty work.

Power issues are once again urgent and volatile in the church. Process theologian Bernard M. Loomer has a remarkable analysis of power in a lecture in social ethics delivered at the University of Chicago (appears as an appendix in Lee, 95, 169–202). This lecture offers substantial insight into servant leadership. One kind of power, the kind most celebrated in dominant U.S. culture, is unilateral. Effects move in one direction. The more a person can have influence while remaining free of influence, the greater the power. Having effects on others is power in the unilateral model.

The alternative is relational power, the capacity to receive effects as well as to have effects. The servant should respond effectively and strongly, but only after having learned what needs exist, only after having received the story of those served. The servant leader is there for the community. The community is not there for the leader.

Leadership in SCCs tends to be collaborative and relational, often as a reaction to the experience of unilateral power in the institutional church. In these small churches the dangerous memory of servant leadership is often full of future content, for themselves, and perhaps for what they offer the larger church.

Religious Hungers

Gallup research over quite a number of years steadfastly documents the religiosity of Americans. Within Catholic culture, workshops and classes in spirituality attract many takers. There have been numerous publications over the last dozen years about lay spirituality and about spirituality in the marketplace. There is keen interest in learning more about the Bible. But church attendance is very low, and younger people are not a large part of those who do show up. This is a painful reality for Catholicism because till now "Mass" has always been an utterly central experience in Catholic culture.

Liturgy is familiar ritual that has elements of utter predictability as well as freshness in each expression. The balance between predictability and freshness is tenuous in times of upheaval. We probably all tire of hearing that we live in an in-between time. Consider the language familiar to those of us "of a certain age":

"What Mass are you going to?"

"I heard the 8:30 Mass."

"Who said the Mass?" or "Who had the Mass?"

For centuries Mass was "said" in Latin for people who neither spoke nor understood it; it was clear that the priest who spoke the Latin was the one who "said" the Mass. Throughout the whole of the church, people saw only the backs of those in front of them, except for the priest who saw no one. There was nothing that any person "attending Mass" was expected to do except to be there.

Contrast this with the directives of Vatican II on Liturgy that there should always be "full active participation" on the part of all of those present. Full active participation means a ritual behavior entirely in opposition to "hearing Mass." It takes time to develop a different ritual history. In fact, the expression "ritual history" is redundant. Ritual works because people have lived into it and have embedded it in their instincts. That happens only through thick historical time. A congregation with six hundred people does not suddenly—perhaps not even in a single generation—create a new instinctive behavioral history: full, active participation. Size is not the only drawback, but it does make a huge difference. One of the most consistent patterns in SCCs is the full active participation of all of the members when the community gathers. A new history is accumulating.

Full active participation does not mean merely participating in what the presider does. That still falls short. The community itself should be the liturgical subject. In fact, in the early church, community leadership came first, and whoever presided in the community's life also presided in the community's Eucharist, for that was part of its essential life. (This was affirmed in two memoranda sent by the Central Theological Commission to the bishops working on *Lumen Gentium* in Vatican II.) SCCs probably don't consciously think that the nature of community itself is their liturgical subject, but their behaviors are moving in that direction, especially in celebration of the Word. A black pastor in New Orleans often says to the congregation: "You are not the audience. You are the performance." That happens far more easily in an SCC than in a traditional parish, so we might do well to consult the lived experience of SCCs.

What is at stake here in Catholic culture is a reclaiming of the centrality of the community as people of God. For example, in the Rite of Christian Initiation for Adults (RCIA), it is clear that responsibility for forming new members into a Catholic faith belongs above all not just *to* the community but *in* the community. There is fruitful exploration afoot, especially in the North American Forum for Small Christian Communities, about the catechumenal possibilities of SCCs, since the initiation model is based upon the dynamics of socialization rather than indoctrination (though initiation into a belief structure is important as well).

The emphasis in the Tridentine eucharistic ritual was upon the transcendence of God, a sense of deity reinforced by the soaring, eye-lifting lines of Gothic church architecture. With liturgical reform came a rearrangement of liturgical space. The altar is renamed the table and is placed *in* the community, rather than against a wall. Community members greet and speak at the sign of peace. The language of the entire celebration is familiar, that is, in the vernacular. Communicants take the cup and hold the consecrated bread in their hands. These changes place more emphasis upon God as immanent.

There has been strong disruption of community over this retrieval of immanence and its relation to what many feel has been a loss of transcendence. Battles over the removal or retention of the communion rail have been commonplace. Removing that structure changes the relationship between sacred space (where altar, tabernacle, priest, and altar servers are) and profane space (where the community gathers). The line of demarcation is lowered. The communion rail battle is about an interpretation of who God is and where God is to be found, where sacred space is located: Is God more likely to be encountered in sacred space, or does space become sacred when God has been encountered there?

When it registers for King David that he lives in a magnificent palace while the Ark of the Covenant is simply shaded under an awning, he decides to build a lavish temple for Yahweh. But Yahweh balks at this and has Nathan remind David that Yahweh always chooses to pitch a tent wherever Yahweh's people pitch their tents. Yahweh is content to continue traveling with only a tent. "Holy" is wherever the people are and Yahweh is with them.

The theological task for the church today is to affirm that "with us" (immanence) and "beyond us" (transcendence) are coordinate experiences. We can only experience God on the basis of God's being with us. God is always more than we experience, but the only clues we have to the "more than" are those intimations that glimmer through God's being with us. It is our surmise that SCCs might provide the faith experience that can fund a new theological understanding of the internal relationship between immanence and transcendence in religious experience.

We have named the religious context of Catholic culture in the U.S. in two ways. The first is the transformation that recentralizes community and recognizes the whole community as a liturgical subject. The second is a serious question about religious experience: who God is and, because of who God is, where and how the encounter between God and us takes place.

In the ritual life of small Christian communities, there is usually a transparent experience of full, active participation. And the fact that they tend to meet other than on "church property" also makes a statement about sacred space. "House church" is a healthy reminder about the "where" of God.

Closing

Understanding how we understand is the business of hermeneutics. We always understand from where we are, who we are, what our history is, what our language is, what our loves and hates are, and so on. While it is always possible for us to transcend local limitation to a degree, we can never fully take leave of the local situations in which we live and move and have our being.

Small Christian communities are a worldwide phenomenon, with their own diverse regional, national, and continental appropriations of this experience of church. In this chapter we've explored some aspects of SCCs with a keen awareness of the local situations within the "U.S. Catholic Church," for these frame our scope and our limitations.

3

The Churchhood of Small Christian Communities: Claiming Ecclesiality

Introduction

Churchhood is important to small Christian communities because it gives their participation in the conversation called church a constitutive role (along with other voices, of course). It could perhaps be told as well in the opposite direction: being a voice in the constitutive conversation confirms small Christian communities' churchhood.

In this chapter we attend to the issue of churchhood for SCCs. We first consider three papal exhortations following the recent Continental Synods. We look at the "Word" ecclesiology of Paul's Letter to the Romans. It will then be useful to speak of a distinction between mainstream and marginal churchhood, although we insist that "margins" are still "on the page" and are often where newness first makes an appearance. We then look at four descriptors that normally accompany churchhood. And finally we will see how scale affects what ecclesial units can at times do well (or do poorly if the size doesn't fit the activity).

Papal Exhortations

After the synods in Asia, Africa, and America, the pope's exhortations to the respective churches give both high praise for small church communities and also constant reminders that church communion is necessary. There is always the fear that small groups can polarize and divide. That does not seem to have been the SCC experience, but the caution is well taken. These synod documents will influence how the church unfolds in the proximate and perhaps longer-term future.

Small church communities are an important experience in many parts of Africa. The African bishops have often promoted them for pastoral reasons. In some parishes in Kenya, for example, the coordinators of SCCs constitute the parish council, a way of assuring that the council is profoundly in touch with the experience of the people. In the exhortation after the African Synod, *Ecclesia in Africa*, the pope says:

> Right from the beginning, the synod fathers recognized that the church as family cannot reach her full potential unless she is divided into communities small enough to foster close human relationships. The assembly described the characteristics of such communities as follows: Primarily they should be places engaged in evangelizing themselves, so that subsequently they can bring the good news to others; they should moreover be communities which pray and listen to God's word, encourage the members themselves to take on responsibility, learn to live an ecclesial life, and reflect on different human problems in the light of the Gospel. Above all, these communities are to be committed to living Christ's love for everybody, a love which transcends the limits of the natural solidarity of clans, tribes, or other interest groups. (§89)

By way of implementation, in a later section the pope asks all dioceses to set up justice and peace commissions and clearly describes critical components of faith's public life:

> All persons, according to their state of life, should be especially trained to know their rights and duties, the meaning of service to the common good, honest management of goods and the proper manner of participating in political life, in order to be able to act in a credible manner in the face of social injustices..... In the pluralistic societies of our day, it is especially due to the commitment of Catholics in public life that the church can exercise a positive influence.

Whether they be professionals or teachers, business people or civil servants, law enforcement agents or politicians, Catholics are expected to bear witness to goodness, truth, justice, and love of God in their daily life. (§§107, 108)

One of the important contributions of SCCs is that they are a place where the dialogue between experience and faith clarifies for Catholics the implications of their faith for both their inner life and their transformative public vocation.

The exhortation *Ecclesia in Asia* recalls that small communities were the shape of the early church, and it encourages particular attention to the processes and dynamics of communion among and between churches. In the context of concern for the involvement of laity in pastoral planning and for the involvement of youth, the pope writes:

In this context and drawing on their pastoral experience, the synod fathers underlined the value of basic ecclesial communities as an effective way of promoting communion and participation in parishes and dioceses, and as a genuine force for evangelization. These small groups help the faithful to live as believing, praying, and loving communities like the early Christians (Acts 2:44–47; 4:32–35). They aim to help their members to live in a spirit of fraternal love and service, and are therefore a solid starting point for building a new society, the expression of a civilization of love....I encourage the church in Asia, where possible, to consider these basic communities as a positive feature of the church's evangelizing activity. At the same time, they will only be truly effective if—as Pope Paul VI wrote—they live in communion with the particular and universal church, in heartfelt communion with the church's pastors and with the magisterium, with a commitment to missionary outreach.... (§25)

Again we hear about the importance of the inner life of SCCs in internal evangelization and of their public life as a starting point for building a new world. There is also expressed a strong concern for communion of the small churches with the larger church. Even Paul had to remind house churches that they didn't belong to their founders or leaders, but to Christ (1 Cor 1:11–16).

What Pope John Paul II says to the Asian churches in general about communion applies, *mutatis mutandis*, to SCCs: "Communion calls for mutual understanding and a coordinated approach to mission, without prejudice to the autonomy and rights of the churches according to their respective theological, liturgical, and spiritual traditions" (§26).

The exhortation following the Synod of America, *Ecclesia in America*, speaks of SCCs with a particular emphasis upon their importance to parish life:

> One way of renewing parishes, especially urgent for parishes in large cities, might be to consider the parish as a community of communities and movements. It seems timely therefore to form ecclesial communities and groups of a size that allows for true human relationships.... In such a human context it will be easier to hear the word of God, to reflect on the range of human problems in the light of this word and gradually to make responsible decisions inspired by the all-embracing love of Christ. (§41)

In *Redemptoris Missio*, the pope also observed that base communities help decentralize the parish (§51). Because so much internal ministry occurs in SCCs, there is less central concern needed in a parish to attend to many forms of ministry to individual members.

The dynamics named repeatedly are the benefits of a small group so that people get to know each other and bond with members. The research on U.S. communities indicates that the sense of belonging to a small church community tends to increase ownership of the larger parish community (Lee, 2000, 105). The possibility of discussion in a small group promotes open dialogue between people's lives and the Word, the kind of appropriation of meaning and resolve that is very difficult in a group the size of a regular parish Eucharist.

Recurring themes in the pope's responses to the Continental Synods are:

1. recognition of the importance of small groupings
   where the experience of people gathered is cherished
   by the community;
2. the importance of probing the scriptures in small
   groups where the correlation with people's experience
   is more immediate and personal;
3. the internal evangelization that occurs from the small
   group processing of scripture;
4. the external evangelization when the small group
   addresses social situations that affect them;
5. the ecclesial nature of these activities, leading to naming such small groups small *church* communities; and—
6. the importance of communion among small communities with the local church and, through the local
   church, with the universal church.

A papal exhortation following the European Synod is not yet available through the documentation series *Origins*.

There have been four Congresses of European Small Christian Communities, and planning has begun for the next one. These have been organized by the communities themselves. At the fourth congress, held in 1991 at Antony, a suburb of Paris, major themes were named through a consultation process. There was much concern for how the European economic community (EEC) would impact upon the poor of Europe, and how it might further marginalize Africa, as U.S. economic policies have marginalized much of Latin America. Another theme was the importance of an accurate reading of scripture.

One of the great surprises of the congress was the presence of representatives from SCCs or house churches that functioned for many years behind the Iron Curtain. In August of 1999 the Iona Community in Scotland hosted a conference of SCC representatives from central and eastern Europe. They came from Poland, Lithuania, the Czech Republic, Slovakia, Ukraine, Hungary, and Yugoslavia. In his unpublished report on the conference, Ian Fraser, Iona Community member and conference organizer, noted the central importance of scripture in the life of these SCCs. They named the "freshness involved in interpreting the Gospel in a way which is continually, flexibly related to people's experience, needs, etc."

They also named their sense that when they meet in community "we are the church now." They said that SCCs avoided the "danger of putting energy into the survival model church."

The attention these SCCs paid to economic factors, wrote Fraser, deserves attention:

> There is a need for an economics based on sustainability rather than growth, which produces effective economic policies leading to shared resources and which do not exclude the poor or those from poorer countries. Such a form of economic partnership and development would form an effective counterbalance to the USA and combat the multi-national companies. Economic policies should also encourage effective environmental legislation as well as providing access to new technologies.

It is clear to these communities that God's intentions for a just world require that faith show a public as well as a private face.

In Latin America there has been much support and encouragement for SCCs shown in the Medellin, Puebla, and Santo Domingo documents. There are differences in the U.S. Hispanic experience of SCCs since Catholics are a minority in the U.S., just as Hispanics are a minority (though a sizable, growing, and very significant minority). In 1989 the U.S. Bishops' Committee on Hispanic Affairs issued *Communion and Mission*, a guide for bishops and pastoral leaders on small Church communities. These communities evangelize their members, of course, and they also help preserve the richness of Hispanic culture:

> Small church communities strengthen Hispanic religiosity—a homespun spirituality that enables them to take responsibility for their Christian way of living....Small communities fortify a centuries-old tradition of faith. Affirmed and strengthened in their identity as Catholics, Hispanics can better serve the larger community. Yet while small communities serve to preserve a vibrant faith, they are not simply warehouses of religious and cultural traditions. They are truly the expression of an emerging spirituality.

We continue this discussion of churchhood by acknowledging its complexity.

Some Graced Theological Ambiguity

All small communities are small groups, but not all small groups are small communities. Community is a deeper, more inclusive, more demanding, and more rewarding kind of reality than many small groups. No one, however, can "start" a small community. We start small groups, and if the right things happen, the small group may become a small community. The process is slow and organic. It takes time, and there is no exact moment when a group is no longer just a small group, but suddenly a community.

There are analogous issues around becoming church, or even becoming Christian. If a person from an altogether different religious tradition chooses to become Catholic, RCIA is (if done well) a solid starting point. The rites of initiation mark a genuine sort of "induction," but it is truly just an initiation and not a consummation. One has to live a long time in a new culture before that culture's deep story imbues the heart and mind with values and instinctive comportment.

When communion ecclesiology is articulated, it is more apt to come from people with vested interests in the effective life of the church as institution. The concerns are exactly right, and there are pastoral exigencies in affirming them. In his recent book *Christian Sacraments in a Postmodern World*, Kenan Osborne addresses issues related to the notion of the church as foundational sacrament (Osborne, 1999, 112–14). He notes, simply and importantly, that in some of the documents of Vatican II, churchhood is attributed to traditions that are not in union with Rome. One of the sections of the document on *Eastern Churches* is titled "Relations with the Brethren of Separated Churches." In the Vatican II document on *Ecumenism*, chapter 3 is entitled "Churches and Ecclesial Communities Separated from the Roman Apostolic See." And in 1982, in a joint statement issued by John Paul II and Robert Runcie, Archbishop of Canterbury, we read that "The bond of our common baptism into Christ led our predecessors to inaugurate a serious dialogue between our churches...." There is churchhood that accrues to communities of the baptized, whether in union with Rome or not.

The point is not to neglect communion ecclesiology, but to recognize less-explored expressions of communion between baptized Christians who are not Catholic and Catholics. Many SCCs in the U.S. Catholic Church feel their parish connectedness either because there are organizational connections or because all or most of their group members are active in their parishes. Juridical boundary definitions are important, but faithful Gospel discipleship cannot always be confined within them, as documents of Vatican II indicate.

The new Code of Canon Law, for example, affirms that all Catholics have the right to assemble and form associations. SCCs are not oblivious to the church as institution, but they have convictions about the churchhood that is theirs because they are a gathering in discipleship of the baptized. They aren't just borrowing church identity from the larger institution. They exercise the indigenous ownership of the baptized.

Pauline "Word" Ecclesiology

There is a broad New Testament consensus that Christians were not a community distinct from Judaism until the late first century. The pain that is so evident in Matthew's Gospel is not conflict between Christian community and Jewish community, but between two communities within Judaism, one that confesses Jesus as the Messiah, and another that does not. Paul, as an apostle of Jesus Christ, did not think of himself as no longer within Judaism, nor any less a child of Abraham, Isaac, and Jacob. So it is anachronistic to speak of "ecclesiology" in Paul's time as if the issues were the same as now. Still, Paul uses two terms for the "good news" communities. One of them, from which ecclesiology gets its name, is *ekklesia*, which literally means "a gathering of people." The other is *koinonia*, which names the way a group is formed when they *participate* together in its life.

There were no church buildings for centuries in early Christianity. Communities met in people's homes (house churches). In his Letter to the Romans, for example, Paul greets Prisca and Aquila and sends his greetings also "to the church at their house" (Rom 16:5). In his Letter to the Colossians Paul asks that his greetings be given to his "sisters and brothers in Laodicea, and to

Nympha and the church which meets at her house" (Col 4:15). In these early small church communities, the good news gathered them and held them gathered; it sent them and regathered them.

Paul is clear in his Letter to the Romans about the centrality of hearing and responding to the Word to the forming of community:

> But what does it say? "The word is near you, on your lips and in your heart" (that is, the word of faith that we proclaim); because if you confess with your lips that Jesus is Lord and believe in your heart that God raised him from the dead, you will be saved....But how are they to call on one in whom they have not believed? And how are they to believe in one of whom they have never heard? And how are they to hear without someone to proclaim him? And how are they to proclaim him unless they are sent? As it is written, "How beautiful are the feet of those who bring good news!" (Rom 10:8–10, 14–15)

In Hebrew anthropology, the heart is the center of personhood. Paul is saying that it is not simply enough to hear words physically, you must appropriate them, live by them, be captivated by them, have the Word in your heart and in your being. During the homily, someone who presumably is able to interpret the Word accurately suggests to the community the Word's implications for them. The best homilist in the world cannot in ten or fifteen minutes make compelling correlations between the good news and the experience of hundreds of individuals. But a small group of people can grapple with the Word together, help each other name the experience that is accosted by the Word, agree to concrete responses to the Word, and even at times agree to be accountable to the community for responsiveness to the Word.

In the rightly acclaimed *Models of the Church*, Avery Dulles uses the phrase "the church as herald" for the community that becomes church through its response to the Word. The church is not a stable reality—once in existence, always there—writes Dulles. It needs to keep being called into existence through receiving and in turn proclaiming the Word of God. Dulles approvingly cites Karl Barth:

We believe the existence of the Church—which means that we believe each particular congregation of Christ.... *Credo ecclesiam* means that I believe that here, at this place, in this assembly, the work of the Holy Spirit takes place....The Church is not the object of faith, we do not believe *in* the Church; but we do believe that in this congregation the work of the Holy Spirit becomes an event. (Dulles, 1974, 73)

The early churches were called into existence by their responsiveness, guided by the Spirit, to the Word of God. They are truly church that has begun. They are not finished or complete, but they are church. Small communities whose togetherness is compelled principally by the Word are rightly small *church* communities. Churchhood is there. While limited by their size in what they can do and be, they are still church *on scale*.

Mainstream and Marginal: A Continuum

"Mainstream" and "marginal" are relative terms that constitute a spectrum, and the experiences they name are part of any living social organism. These categories can be misused if they are applied narrowly and without nuance since within each category lies ideas, feelings, values, and related behaviors. In settled times in any institution's life, these are not submitted to critical evaluation. A certain amount of change is regularly needed in all institutions, and as long as it does not call the very structure of the institution into serious question, organizational management normally negotiates the needed change. But when widespread structural transformation is needed, when people in central leadership have their own organizational positions called into question, the push and shove for change, the experiment with alternatives, will come from "below" where the critical impulse has more freedom.

In this present discussion, "mainstream" means closer to the energies of ecclesial *societas* or order, and "marginal" means closer to the energies of ecclesial *communitas* or charism. It must also be said at the outset of this discussion that the whole of the small or base Christian community movement, in its great variety of manifestations, runs counter to the way that ecclesial community has been understood and experienced in recent centuries. SCCs are an alternative. Some are closer to mainstream, others are on the edges of wide margins, but in general they have marginal characteristics. The parish that supports Post-Renew communities and the parish that is restructuring itself into a community of communities are both doing something new. It is no secret that there is nervousness about this in the ecclesial *societas* even though cautious support is forthcoming.

By mainstream and marginal we are speaking therefore of *tendencies*, of being more or less one or the other, in short, of experience on a continuum, not either/or.

Mainstream

Mainstream SCCs, in this context, are those communities related to parish life. The most integrally connected are probably those that are part of a restructuring process. For example, the communities inspired by Renew see themselves as functioning within the parish, much as Renew groups functioned within the parish.

There is also a smaller number of SCCs that formed on their own initiative and have no kind of recognition within a parish, but whose members continue to be active in a parish (members might come from several parishes). Parish is where their sacramental life is pitched, and parish is their center of gravity; yet these SCCs meet members' needs that parish life alone would leave unmet.

One strength of these mainstream groups is their support and inventiveness for changing parish life. They are a place where leadership for the larger parish emerges and is schooled. Because of members' attentiveness to needs within the community, ministering occurs that does not require the efforts of the parish team. In this regard parish-based SCCs both reflect and initiate changing patterns in how ministry happens. To be sure, there are *communitas* issues that animate members of SCCs in the parish, the strong desire for something new, dissatisfaction with how needs were met before, and so on. For reasons like that, it is important not to make mainstream and marginal into unambiguously separate orientations.

At the October 1996 International Theological Consultation on Small Christian Communities held at the University of Notre Dame, there was discussion about how SCC leadership should be named. One of the expressions that had support was "animator" (though the French original, *animateur*, carries more punch). In the course of that conversation, several people with parish-connected SCCs said that "animator" was also a good name, not just for community leadership, but for the function of SCCs in a parish. While they never constitute the majority experience, SCCs are sufficiently active and engaged to provide animation for the entire parish. In Tanzania there is a Swahili word for the person who does the spicing of food when it is being prepared. In the singular form, *mkolezati*, that word has become one of the names for the SCC leader, and in the plural form, *wakolezati*, it names how multiple SCCs liven up the whole parish structure. These are examples of how SCCs are perceived in a parish structure to be something like leaven to a mainstream institution.

Marginal

In the interpretation of research on small Christian communities, the notion of "margins" was one of the heuristic devices used, although with hesitancy because of its many commonplace meanings. In terms of resources and power, for example, marginal existence is deplorable. In terms of respect and influence, being marginal is tantamount to being irrelevant. But the word has other meanings.

The metaphor of margins comes from the page, with text in the center and blank space all around. Marginal writings and drawings were commonplace in medieval manuscripts. What is important in this metaphor is that margins are "on the page" and that anyone who reads the page cannot be unaffected by what transpires in the margins. If marginal writing proves durable, it finds its way into later versions of the text.

Think of the church as it is right now as the written text on the page. Then consider all the ways of being church that are possible, but not part of the written text. The margins are the space where the unwritten text interrogates the written text.

During times of great transformation and upheaval, the times between deconstruction and reconstruction, marginal living is critical for the good of us all. Edmond Jabes, a Jewish writer who died over a decade ago, explored the margins metaphor extensively. He said that we should make wide, wide margins because that's where new possibility gets credentialed.

In *Image of the Edge: The Margins of Medieval Art*, Michael Camille says that marginal art exists "in order to give birth to meaning at the center" (1992, 48). Besides examining the marginal art in manuscripts, he also contrasts the sculpture on the outside of great cathedrals (the edges of buildings) with the sculpture and other art inside the edifice. The inside and the outside together complete meaning. Camille illustrates his point from a page of a medieval manuscript of psalms. Whoever copied the manuscript drew a person in the margins who has climbed up the sides of the written text. With one hand he is pointing to a place in the text. In his other hand is a rope, and he is pulling something up with it. As your eyes follow the rope, you see that there are lines of writing below the text, that is, in the bottom margin. The marginal person is showing where, in the main text, the marginal text should be inserted; he's going to pull it up with the rope and put it there. If he succeeds, he will have rewritten the story!

Victor Turner distinguishes between *societas*, that large instance of social life, and *communitas*, a subunit of *societas*. In times of great change, in the liminal period between the before and the after, *communitas* will do much of the probing and experimenting, close as it is to the exigencies of immediate experience. In sociology the comment is made that practice often changes before the law changes to reflect changes in practice. *Communitas* is where some of the new practices are tried out.

Change occurs as the experiments of *communitas* work their way into the innards of *societas* without causing major indigestion. William James described the process of change in regards to an idea: When a major new idea appears, most people say, "It's dangerous, it's untried, it's not orthodox, it should be left alone." But if the idea remains and does well, people are less unnerved by it. They say, "It's not that unusual, what's the big deal, take it or leave it"; but at least they don't actively resist it. In the third stage, when a new idea has in fact been found interesting and fruitful, those who found it dangerous in the first instance now claim to have discovered it.

Let us look at an example of an idea that was first viewed negatively by the church then embraced by it:

In his insistence upon the inviolability of religious conscience, John Courtney Murray was clearly marginal. Less than a century earlier, in *Quanta Cura*, Pius IX called religious conscience an erroneous opinion injurious to the church and to the salvation of souls, and he cited Gregory XVI's judgment that this position was "insane raving." Even as late as the 1950s, Murray's ideas troubled his superiors and his writing was restricted. Yet a relatively short time later, Murray contributed largely to the Vatican II document on religious freedom, which says that every human person has the right to religious freedom.

We think it quite possible, perhaps probable, that small church communities are developing a new and stronger sense of a biblical Catholic identity to complement the long dominance of doctrinal Catholic identity, and that this is fully responsive to the emphasis on God's Word in Vatican II's *Dei Verbum*.

Remaking the Catholic Imagination

In the Catholic imagination, the word "church" often refers to the institutional church. People usually mean the institution when they ask, "Why does the church....?" or "Why doesn't the church....?" They are not questioning themselves. But small Christian communities call themselves church. They are retrieving the Word as a gathering of people, a restored instinctual reference to the people of God, which they and we are.

A second instinctual Catholic usage of "church" commonly signals the physical building. The imposing legacy of the Gothic cathedrals put the church at the village center, with steeples that reached towards the heavens, towering above every other building in the town. The fact that most SCCs do not meet in the parish church also helps intervene in the instinctive connection between "church" and an image of a building. SCCs often meet in members' homes.

While today's SCCs have much in common with the house churches of the early centuries, they are certainly not a mere repetition. House churches were the only option in the beginning. They were the normal form of both ecclesial life and of social life in the Mediterranean first century (the "household"); these forms are all but nonexistent in most nations in the twenty-first century. House churches exist now in a new time for many new reasons.

They reclaim "gathered people" rather than "gathering place" as a fundamental meaning and image for the word "church." How they claim churchhood is an enriching phenomenon for the entire people of God.

In part because familiar meanings of church are in the process of being modified, the issue of churchhood is important and pressing. If church as institution should not be the centerpiece of ecclesial perception, neither should it be marginalized. And if church does not first and foremost name a building, sacred space is no less important. The network of small churches needs a gathering place as much as any individual community.

Churchhood, therefore, is a vital discussion, but raising the issue of the churchhood of the SCCs springing up all over the world is not without problem. The New Testament advice about not putting new wine in old wineskins applies. SCCs are new wine. "Church" has never been a univocal word. It is polyvalent, rich in abundant significations. We should be thankful for the polyvalence for it houses blessed ambiguity about "church" that prevents us from blithely packaging its mystery.

Churchhood Descriptors

In *Dangerous Memories*, we offered a typology for SCCs that many have found useful and we'll discuss again here: *koinonia*, *diakonia*, *kerygma*, and *leitourgia*. These owe a debt to the extremely helpful "models" framework articulated by Avery Dulles—herald, community, servant, sacrament, and institution—although our laying out of these does not exactly follow his use of the models.

In each of the churchhood frameworks that follow we are attempting to be descriptive. It is not a matter of saying that when these models or conditions are fulfilled, you are church. Our starting point, rather, is that when you find what most people recognize as church, you can use these categories to describe what you find. Categories are typological—but "typing" never does justice to any concretely existing reality. We bristle personally at being "type cast," and so does (or ought) church. Mystery is not susceptible to being tamed by typological categories, especially the works of God.

It has become commonplace to cite these descriptors in Anglicized Greek, perhaps for easy reference. Such usage also makes it easier to remember that these are technical, interpretative categories. We'll look at them one by one.

Koinonia

The word itself connects with the notion of participation, and that is a good place to begin. The Gospel is a revelation of God's plan for God's people and of the redemption of human life that comes to all people who are God's people. Redemption itself, as we were reminded in *Lumen Gentium*, has a fundamentally participative character.

In many places, but especially in the latter chapters of 1 Corinthians, Paul reminds Christians that they are members of one another, that they are all parts of the same body. They don't *become* connected when they choose to behave in certain ways. Through baptism they are already connected. The only question is how powerfully they will honor all the ways in which they participate in each other's reality. SCCs are a place where lives rub up against each other in near enough ways that this truth stands a solid chance of capturing human consciousness and behavior.

We want to offer a short bracket about our use of the social sciences in theological reflection. When David Tracy says that Catholics have an "analogical imagination," he names our tendency to emphasize how the world is like God who made it and how the world mediates our experience of God. We know that sin is there too, but we have confidence that the analogical likenesses super-abound. He contrasts this with a "dialectic imagination" which is preoccupied with the great gulf between the world and God and dwells upon how unlike God is to our soiled, creaturely experience. He says there are no pure types, no one who is only analogical or only dialectic, but that these are marked tendencies. Because of our analogical imagination, sacrament is especially important for Catholics. A world that, in Gerald Manley Hopkins' words, "is charged with the grandeur of God" is a world able to mediate religious experience.

Contemporary Catholic theology is often disposed to have the human sciences as partners in reflection upon religious experience. Marriage is already a Hebrew Bible metaphor for God's relationship with Israel. By the end of the first Christian millennium, Catholic experience had begun to reckon marriage as a sacrament. We would add that a solid, loving marriage mediates our experience of God's love for us. A poor marriage cannot mediate that experience. We can describe a "good marriage" in religious language, and we can also use the language of the social sciences to say what is healthy and functional and what is disabling and dysfunctional. We can use the language of organization and management to describe healthy ways for power to function in human community, or we can use metaphors that Jesus uses for leadership (servant, for example). The conversation between theology and the social sciences is particularly important to people like Catholics who are at home with an analogical imagination.

As we speak about *koinonia* in this book, we can use the language of being members of one another, as Paul does, or we can speak about relationships where mutuality thrives, where reconciliation—never easy—is expected to occur. We can talk about wounding conversation or upbuilding conversation. Having these two languages for religious experience elucidates history's mediation of God's presence. In this book, therefore, there is a lot of moving back and forth between these two languages (a reflection, surely, of the primary disciplines in which the interpretative instincts of the two of us have been incubated!).

Chapter 5, for example, puts at the disposal of a community's inner life much of what we've learned in the twentieth century about conflict resolution, the qualities of good conversation, the dynamics of consensus building, and the redemptive demands of mutuality. Chapter 6 puts at the disposal of a community's public life much of what we've learned about how people are empowered to participate in history.

Koinonia is not only about the way in which community members participate in one another. It is about how communities themselves are connected and how *they* participate in one another. Paul feels the need to scold house churches in Corinth for tending to become idiosyncratic, that is, staying to themselves. No matter who starts the community or who leads it, it does not belong to Apollos or Cephas or Paul even (though Paul makes a special claim). Similarly, it is especially important for communities that are not parish-based to maintain connections so that they do not become Cephas's or Apollos's or Paul's. Forming networks at the local level is one way. Becoming members of one of the national SCC networks and attending regional and national meetings is another way.

Community is an extraordinary grace. Community is necessary and can be of incredible beauty. But no one has ever claimed that community is easy! The dynamics of disparate lives participating in one another is a fearsome task—not nearly so formidable, however, when the journey is "walked out loud" with many companions and with truly ample *koinonia*.

It is worth noting that the kind of Greek in which the New Testament was written is called *koine* Greek, that is, the kind of Greek that people spoke in their daily living as part of their ongoing conversation together. The quality of our conversation and the quality of our community are of a piece. The quality of our conversion and our conversation with God and with each other are also of a piece. In both cases we often put ourselves at risk in the openness needed for genuine conversation. "Conversationriskandconversion" is a very large word.

Diakonia

Diakonia, which means service, comes from the same root as *diakonos*, which means servant. As we noted in the previous chapter, servant is one of the principal metaphors Jesus used for how power should function in community. What a good servant does is respond to need. That presumes that a good servant knows how to look and how to listen in order to assess need accurately. Empathy is one of the most necessary skills in knowing what needs cry out for service in the internal life of an SCC. The ability to engage in social analysis is one of the most necessary skills in knowing what needs cry out for service in the larger community that environs the SCC.

Deep in the Judeo-Christian tradition is the advice that we are to be holy in the way that God is holy. The two recurring clues to the center of divine holiness are justice (*tsedeq*) and mercy (*hesed*). While justice includes many of the legal meanings that it tends to carry in our culture, it is a much more embracing concept in the Hebraic world view. There is an essential rightness about how the world should go, rooted in God's intentions for the world. This rightness sometimes makes an appearance when the Hebrew word *tsedeq* is translated as *righteousness* as well as *justice*.

Hesed names the tender mercies of God as they respond with immediacy to critical, unmet human need. Basic mercy impels the corporal and spiritual works of mercy. We have no choice but to respond swiftly to critical present need. But were that all we did, we would often be empowering an unjust system to endure even longer, since someone is always there to keep picking up the pieces. Those who are committed cooperators with God's intentions for the world are under requirement to intervene in and work to alter unjust social systems responsible for the miseries which mercy must address.

It is easier to engage in works of mercy than in works of justice, that is, the dynamics of systemic change. For reasons that will be laid out in more detail in chapter 5, SCCs as mediating structures in society can be a frontline contact zone for the social justice energies of the church; however, that action requires conversion of consciousness in a culture that likes to keep religion private and in fact "pays" religion, through tax-exemption laws, to keep out of public life.

Some SCCs begin their meetings ritually with "the news." For a few minutes during each gathering, a member uses newspapers, news magazines, religious publications, and so on, to say, "Here are events that happened since we last met: world events, national events, local events." Such a brief news time helps a community have wider eyes. Some communities add on to this their own news, making time for members to tell their own stories. Others alternate personal news and world news at different gatherings. The personal news gives community members a chance to share experiences that they feel are important. Sometimes much has happened since the last meeting. Sometimes a little. Sometimes someone says, "I pass. It's been a very ordinary week or two."

It is the obligation of any Christian community to service need within the community and beyond the community. A community needs to develop its own "listening devices" in order to assess need. *Diakonia* is a natural consequence of *koinonia*. If we are members of one another, the needs of the community and the resources of the community must connect.

Kerygma

Kerygma gives small communities their essential definition as small *Christian* communities. The *kerygma* is the message of Jesus

Christ, the announcement of the reign of God, the good news. In one of its earliest names, it is simply "the Way."

If the *kerygma* was called the Way or the good news, there had to be reasons why the experience was so named. And these are not the only names for the experience that the post-Easter communities used. New Testament scholarship generally agrees that teacher and prophet were probably used of Jesus in his lifetime, but that most of the Christological ways of naming Jesus were conferred by the believing community after Easter. Each title reflects a community's particular experience of Jesus in their lives. In the Jesus-event, God did something for them that they could not do for themselves.

The New Testament is like Elizabeth Barrett Browning's sonnet to her husband in which she asks, "How Do I Love Thee?" She replies to her own question, "Let me count the ways." And then beautiful images pour out, one after another, to tell of her love. The titles of Jesus in the New Testament were not assembled systematically. They rose up out of particular concrete experiences of Jesus. "How do I love thee? Let me count the ways. Thou art the Christ, the Messiah. Thou art the Son of Man. Thou art the Son of God. Thou art the Son of David. Thou art Lord. Thou art High Priest. Thou art Second Adam. Thou art King of the Jews. Thou art Truth. Thou art Life. Thou are Light." This is Christological poetry.

To call these names for Jesus "Christological" is to reach into the Jewish experience of being anointed. The Greek word from which we have "Christ" in English simply means anointed, one who has had oil poured on one. The anglicized Hebrew word for the same thing is *Messiah*. Kings and prophets were anointed, special ones. Israel experienced something that it needed to be saved from and yet could not seem to save itself from; it relied on God's promise that an anointed one would do for the people what they could not do for themselves.

Kerygma is about what God does for us in the Jesus-event that we need done and yet cannot do for ourselves. *Soter* is the Greek word for savior, and *soteriology* is the theology of what we need to be saved from and how God works through Jesus in the Spirit to save us. Soteriology is at the center of Christology. If Jesus is experienced as the Messiah, what is it that he does for us that we need to have done and yet cannot do for ourselves? What happened to people's lived experience in those earliest years that made them call the Jesus-event the best good news they'd ever heard, so good they'd die for it as well as live for it?

A recent study by Notre Dame sociologists puts regular Catholic attendance at Sunday Eucharist at about 27 percent. If Catholics are absenting themselves from church participation in large numbers, is this not a matter of relevance? Time at church does not connect faith and lived experience in a way that is "clearly good" for that lived experience.

We begin the next chapter by saying that SCCs are a privileged place for the doing of theology. Theology often has the ring of an esoteric, academic enterprise. But like orange juice that "isn't just for breakfast anymore," theology is not just for the academy anymore and never should have been. It is organized reflection on the experience of faith by people of faith in communities of faith. Because small communities are such a primary contact zone with lived experience for church, they ought to be a home for theologizing a new soteriology. Members of SCCs are showing up for (house) church, and something is addressing them that makes them turn up. *Kerygma* gathers them in the first place, but it is also taking shape anew at a time when old answers are often not interactive with today's questions—or if they are, not in traditional forms.

The issue is more of an existential soteriology: what difference does or can Jesus Christ make to me, to us? What formulation of the *kerygma* can make its soteriological relevance incandescent? We express our hope that SCCs might help Christian faith reshape its soteriology so that *kerygma* regains a reputation for being unmistakably good news.

Leitourgia

In its simple original meaning, *leitourgia* named public activity in ancient Greek city life or the public responsibility of wealthier citizens. In Christian life liturgy names the prayer forms that have grown up out of a community's experience, forms that are readily recognizable. Because liturgy is owned by the community, it is one of the means by which communities feel they belong to a life larger than their own.

In the early centuries before there was any such thing as parish structures, house church was the normal way Christians gathered. In Greco-Roman life the household did not mean just the family of parents and children that lived in the same house, but a wider relational group of servants, clients, close friends, and so on. When the bishops were working on the Vatican II dogmatic constitution on the church, *Lumen Gentium*, the Central Theological Commission forwarded two similar memoranda reminding them that, in the early church, those who led the community also presided over its Eucharist (Legrand, 1979, 413-14). Laying on hands validated a person's leadership in the community, in virtue of which that same person became the natural one to lead Eucharist. In later centuries the relationship was reversed: the laying on of hands conferred the power to preside at Eucharist in virtue of which the ordained person would lead a community.

It's either an exquisite irony or a work of God's Spirit that, as the numbers of small communities mount, the number of the ordained diminishes. Christian communities regularly having Eucharist was no problem for the early centuries. But that is not where we are today! The dangerous memory of ancient Eucharist tradition, however, perhaps holds future content.

Since most SCCs in the U.S. Catholic Church are parish-connected, members ordinarily participate in the parish Mass, but they do not regularly go together as SCC members. Their principal activity as a community is around scripture and prayer. A small number of Eucharist-centered communities regularly have Eucharist, most often by inviting priests to preside; a few have the same priest as a regular presider.

Many of the SCCs that are not parish-based and do not have Eucharist will nonetheless have breaking of bread and sharing of a cup as part of their regular ritual to maintain their orientation toward the Lord's Supper. Some will say it's eucharist with a small "e" so as to make clear that they are not confusing their memorial with formal Eucharist. Scripture plays the central ritual role in most of these grassroots communities.

In *Dangerous Memories*, under the topic of *leitourgia*, we reflected upon Eucharist. Based upon emerging trends since then, we want to note the very important role that the Liturgy of the Word plays in the life of SCCs. We would like to allude to a position developed more fully in *The Future Church of 140 BCE*, that since the mid-sixties Catholics have begun a retrieval of scripture that hints at a new experience of two real presences, not just that of Eucharist (Lee, 1995, 151–55).

Real presence is redundant. Either it's real or it isn't presence. "Real" is a way of naming a "privileged" or "most important" or "utterly central" experience of God's immediate, active presence through Jesus Christ in the Eucharist. Edward Schillebeeckx has enriched the discussion of presence with the idea of "density." The Christ-event is there for human history all the time. It is never missing. The issue then is not presence or absence, but density of presence. Every presence of God is mediated by the world and by events. To call eucharistic presence a "real presence" is then a testimony to the centrality of Eucharist, a density of presence, in mediating the Catholic experience of Jesus Christ.

Many Catholics recall that the Mass was once "divided" into three principal parts: the offertory, consecration, and communion. To fulfill one's obligation it was necessary to be at all three parts. If you missed the first part, you could stay that far into the next Mass, but if you missed two parts, you had to remain for the entirety of the next Mass. What is interesting in retrospect is that the liturgy of the Word did not even count! Sermons were expected not to exceed ten minutes, and they were rarely of the sort that were genuinely insightful into the biblical text and that text's relevancy to the concrete lived experience of those assembled.

The piety and liturgical life of more and more Catholics are changing as they discover the Bible again, along with a veritable mine of scholarship that's becoming available at the popular level. When SCCs give a central place to scripture, it is no longer the ten-minute version. Probing scriptures is a sustained and organized conversation between Word and world. It often takes place with the help of a good commentary and seldom takes less than an hour, often even twice that. The probing often has social analysis as a conversational dialogue partner: what has this story to do with our story? In what ways is our lived experience accosted by God's Word? The words of the sacred story are not there just for remembering a past event, but for chasing down present events; even more, the words are not fully "Word" until they confront present events. We know at that point that we have been addressed by the living God, and that too is real presence. It is not interchangeable with the real presence of the Eucharist and is not meant to replace it. Those who cannot have Eucharist but can have Word know they are not without real presence of the living God.

Because of Catholic culture's love affair with the Eucharist, the liturgy of the Word may seem like a poor substitute for the real thing when there is no priest. It should never be a substitute, but it is, in fact, a different yet equally shattering experience of presence, not in its old ten-minute sermon form, but in its new form of sustained dialogue with experience. A positive benefit is that the Word takes the pressure off the Eucharist to be almost everything. In its origins, the Eucharist on the Lord's Day celebrated the power of Jesus' death and resurrection within a community's life. It was the high point of the week. When Eucharist became a daily devotion rather than a central Sunday event, the specialness of Sunday could not but suffer. It may be that a new kind of rhythm between Liturgy of the Word and Liturgy of the Eucharist is an experiment in the name of the whole church that is being carried on in small Christian communities.

In any event, Liturgy of the Word belongs to Catholic *leitourgia*. When trying to understand their churchhood, SCCs now know that the Word as well as the Eucharist is a shared form of public liturgy and, as such, expresses their churchhood.

Canon Law affirms the right of all Christians to assemble and form associations. Our baptism empowers us to do that. Like Schillebeeckx's notion of "density" in respect to eucharistic presence, the four characteristics named above can help SCCs reflect upon the density of their ecclesiality.

The Small "Scale" Advantages of SCCs

Most people who go to church regularly do not have explicit, regular contact with other Catholics outside the Sunday parish assembly. Yet the relational scale of an ordinary Sunday assembly does not elicit some of the very formative dynamics that only a smaller scale can facilitate. In this section we will attend to the issue of scale in ecclesial culture and to contributions of SCCs because of the scale in which they are church. By scale we mean proportionality. Some things are best done by large groups, others best done by small groups. Relative size impacts upon what a group can do well, less well, or even not at all.

We will look at scale first in the context of Eucharist and eucharistic community, second in respect to what we will call the homiletic function in smaller scale gatherings, and finally in the way in which attachment to a smaller unit furthers attachment to the larger unit in which the smaller is located. By homiletic function we mean whatever connects Word and lived experience in such ways that meaning emerges and that concrete responses are elicited. Some things can happen when the Word is appropriated in a small group that are not possible when a large group hears a homily from someone who is not a regular participant in that group's experience.

Scale and Eucharistic Community

We've already mentioned that SCCs have much in common with the small church communities in Paul's time. They listen to the good news (though there were not yet any fixed gospel texts in Paul's time). They gather in homes large enough to accommodate the group. They evangelize internally; and we know that they also evangelize externally, for their numbers grow with amazing speed. In fact, it should perhaps be expected that the mission of any small church community would include generating other communities.

The most notable difference between Paul's time and our own is that most SCCs do not celebrate Eucharist in their gatherings, except for Eucharist-centered communities. (Eucharist-centered communities are less than one percent of the total number and do not celebrate Eucharist within their SCC as a function of the current ecclesial system.)

The upside of this arrangement is that celebrating Sunday Eucharist in the parish, which is what most community members do, keeps SCCs vitally connected to the parish. SCC members are also significantly more active in the parish than members of the general Catholic population. The downside of this arrangement is perhaps the upside of that small (but not insignificant) number of Eucharist-centered communities, for the research data clearly shows that Eucharist-centered communities have the greatest longevity.

Although the research did not get at this issue directly, we would guess that Eucharist gives these communities a further fullness that in turn fosters their long life.

A true church community is by apostolic character a eucharistic community, and it makes sense that the one who presides over the community's life also and naturally presides at its Eucharist. There is nothing scriptural, or theological, or pastorally practical that would prevent the church from allowing this and ordaining leaders of SCCs to preside at Eucharist. We do not, however, expect that to happen, for it would require a huge new systemic structure that would redefine the role of parishes and dioceses and beg for a re-theologizing of the sacrament of orders. But it is a marginal possibility, one evoked by marginal ecclesial life. And the great value of margins, as we've said, is that they are still part of the page.

There is a liturgical dictum that no one should be seen doing any liturgical ministry that she/he is not seen doing within the community outside the liturgy (Kavanagh, 1982, 12). If that applies to leadership as well, then it makes consummate good sense that the one who plays a key role in leading the community regularly would also preside over the community's liturgy. This is a matter of scale that makes it functionally possible to connect the daily lived experience of a community to its ritual life. Then, when the presider prays in the name of the community, the community will clearly recognize that those are *its* prayers. Then their "Amen" will truly mean, "Yes, since our presider got it exactly right, Lord, hear *our* prayer." Church on a small scale makes this kind of leading and praying more likely. It is not the failure of the presider to do this when the assembly numbers five hundred or a thousand. On that scale it is just not possible. Unfortunately, because of the lack of ordained priests today, many parishes are being linked in ministry with other parishes or fully conjoined into a single parish.

The National Alliance of Parishes Restructuring into Communities is a development in the U.S. Catholic Church spearheaded by Fr. Art Baranowski of the Detroit Archdiocese. Fr. Baranowski regularly insists that what the National Alliance proposes is not a parish program to initiate and support small church communities, but a different way altogether of structuring a parish. Such a full restructuring would, of course, require time, reeducation, and infinite patience. We would invite you, however, to reread the already cited texts of the pope's encouraging support of small church communities. The larger church has perhaps been readied by contemporary circumstances to rethink its micro-level structures, as well as its larger institutional structures.

We would like to see the National Alliance and the Eucharist-centered communities get their notes together in the margins of the "manuscript" called church!

To continue this reflection on scale, we will consider Paul's words in his First Letter to the Corinthians:

> Now in the following instructions I do not commend you, because when you come together it is not for the better but for the worse....When you come together, it is not really to eat the Lord's supper. For when the time comes to eat, each of you goes ahead with your own supper, and one goes hungry and another becomes drunk. What! Do you not have homes to eat and drink in?...Examine yourselves, and only then eat of the bread and drink of the cup. For all who eat and drink without discerning the body, eat and drink judgment against themselves....Now you are the body of Christ and individually members of it. (Cor 11:17, 20–22a, 28–29; 12:27)

When Paul tells the Corinthians that they do not recognize the body of Christ, he does not seem to be inplying that they miss the reality of the bread and the cup, but that their *behavior* does not recognize the body of Christ that they are. John Haughey insists upon the essential relationship between the "social flesh" of the body of Christ which the community is and the reality of Christ in the breaking of the bread and the sharing of the cup. The gathering to which the passage refers is a double ritual: a shared meal and the Eucharist. "They conveniently sacramentalized the second part while allowing their pre-member, unconverted sociality to be evident in the first part....The sacramental and the social, rather than being two sides of one reality, stood in contradiction to one another in Corinth" (Haughey, 1980, 188, 120).

The pastoral and ritual point we want to make is that Paul's ability to recognize and name community failures depends upon there being a community where there are enough observable interactions that success and failures in Christian community are palpable.

Except possibly for the few remaining rural parishes in this country, there is seldom enough sustained interaction among those who participate in a Sunday parish Eucharist for them to be called by the ritual of Eucharist to deal with their issues, obligations, and possibilities as an identifiable group of people. Without such regular contact and interaction, parish members cannot experience the pressure and/or grace of being the body of Christ. And that is what justifies eating together the same bread and drinking from the same cup. The kiss of peace is frequently a ritual part of an SCC's life. If reconciliation in the community is needed, that need is felt keenly at the kiss of peace. It tells an important truth, because the scale is there to disclose the dynamics of the community's relational life.

We want to be clear that Eucharist does not belong only or always in the same small church group. We are always members of a parish and a larger local church whom our bishop leads. And our local church is likewise always part of the universal church whose integral life together is signaled by the leadership of the bishop of Rome. Because all of these units are church, built up out of smaller units of church, Eucharist tells the truth at every level.

Scale and Liturgy of the Word Community

The "Word of God" names the perception of God's communication with us in many ways. When the prophets say that the Word of God came to them, they are telling the people of their conviction, born of their relationship with God, about what God expects the world to look like and what in turn people's collaboration with God needs to look like. At other times we proclaim the scriptures and then say, "The Word of God." Still other times, after rigorous discernment, an individual says, "I believe deeply that this is what God wants me to do. And when God speaks, I try to respond."

In the reflections that follow, we presume that the Word of God has always been, and in its fullest sense still is, God's "word of address" to a present situation. When the angel of God spoke to Mary, it addressed her immediate situation. When we hear the record of a past Word, our task is to ask how that text addresses our present moment. It may be "word" when it is a record of God having spoken, and it is not incorrect, therefore, to call it the Word of God. But it truly comes to life as *Word* with a capital "*W*" when the hearing of it confronts and addresses immediate lived experience.

The homiletic function tries to enable the biblical text to speak as well as possible with its original voice to our present experience. This calls for a strong dialogue between our interpretations of the biblical text and our interpretations of our immediate situation. In his book on the character of a true biblical community, Paul Hanson says there is always a double exegesis of Word and world (Hanson, 1987, 529). If we get Word right and world wrong, we are in serious trouble. And the trouble is just as serious if we get world right and Word wrong.

We know from educational models, especially in adult education, that participation in a process that arrives at a solution or a commitment has far different results than simply being told what needs to be done. Those of us who are homilists often feel stranded or "abstract" when we have very little knowledge of a community we are addressing. To be sure, there are great pressing issues that touch everyone, and these can be named in effective ways with which most people identify and name as their own. But even when we know a community fairly well, we can suggest very little that has the sting of the real since there is a such a variety of persons and experiences before us. We do not know who is happy, who is in turmoil, who is facing death or divorce or abandonment, who is in a new love or an old hatred, whose social world is gleaming and whose is deteriorating, who sees the world from a liberal or moderate or conservative lens, and so on.

In the formal celebration of Eucharist, only ordained presbyters and deacons are allowed to give homilies on biblical texts. In small church communities, the homiletic function belongs to the community in a way that can occur only on a small scale. There is often a facilitator of the celebration of the Word, and there are helpful materials published for SCCs for leading a conversation with a text. These resources often foreground a text before it is heard, and sometimes foreground interpretations of present experience that help the conversation between Word and world get off to a good start.

If there is a kind of faith "magic" that animates SCCs, we would say that it is the ritual way in which everyone participating in naming the world of experience becomes a conversation partner with Word. This is an active, collective process that gives the appropriation of meaning its best chance. With an average size of thirteen adults, most SCCs draw everyone into the homiletic discernment process.

What the research on SCCs shows is that these communities are better at interpreting what the conversation between Word and world means for its members' inner life than for the community's public life. If we can find a way to bring the church's social teaching into the dialogue, SCCs may help this teaching be implemented in ways heretofore not possible.

There is also a relationship between commitment and scale. Empirically, SCC members have a significantly stronger attachment to church and involvement in church ministries than the general Catholic population (Lee, 2000, 62–63). We think that Edmund Burke's military metaphor is operative here: "To be attached to the subdivision, to love the little platoon we belong to in society [is] the first principle, the germ as it were of public affections. It is the first link in the services by which we proceed towards a love to our country and to mankind" (cited in Pelikan, 1992, 139). Membership in the small group helps this attachment occur if attachment to the larger group is articulated and ritualized.

Closing

In the U.S. Catholic Church, parish life has a long history that is solid, supportive, and strong. Closely allied with parish life has been a vast system of Catholic schools in which the cultural identity of millions of Catholics has been formed. For most of their history, nearly all of those schools, whether parish-related or private, have been under the sponsorship and direction of religious orders. In the 1950s, half of all the Roman Catholic seminarians in the world were in the United States. Parishes had many young priests with appeal to young Catholics, and religious communities had many young members in their schools and hospitals. Because of that strong, good Catholic history, many of us remember church instinctively in those categories: vibrant parishes, strong schools, competent hospital care. However, as many familiar, identity-forming structures are coming loose at the seams, we are thrown back upon our resources to reimagine the meaning of churchhood.

In this chapter we looked through the vistas of *koinonia, diakonia, kerygma* and *leitourgia* as a way of trafficking with the dangerous memories of an early time when there was indeed church, but few of its institutions were forms of church life later familiar to most of us. There is future content in the sense that a past which differs from the present suggests the possibility of a future that differs from the present. These four descriptors are not prescriptive, like "one, holy, catholic, and apostolic."

We then looked at the meanings of *mainstream* and *marginal*. We must often remind ourselves that marginal does not mean irrelevant. No society can stay healthy without marginal activity, which facilitates its own pattern of self-transcending. Inasmuch as small Christian community structures have not been the way in which dominant Catholic culture conducted its churchhood in recent centuries, all SCCs, whether parish-connected or not, have a measure of marginality about them. By mainstream SCCs we meant those communities that have a closer relationship with the parish. But, if one can speak of a sort of "sociological theology," we also affirmed the churchhood of more marginal gatherings of Catholics who are still on the page because the margins are part of the page.

Finally we considered the different ways that church is church, depending upon the size of the gathering, that is, the scale of church. We noted that SCCs are church on the small scale, and while there are many aspects of churchhood that are played out on the large scale (dioceses, the universal church), there are also very important ecclesial happenings that require community on the small scale. Many such happenings need small church communities for their reactivation.

4

Gathered and Sent:
Internal and External Mission

Introduction

Matthew's Gospel is especially clear about the discipling process. Discipleship involves being "gatherers of people," using the metaphor of casting fishing nets (Matt 4:18–22). Disciples are to make sure that people's lives are savory ("salted" is the metaphor), and they are to do good works that cast great light and give glory to God (Matt 5:13–16). True disciples are to be informed, not stupid like the one who built a house on sand (Matt 7:24–27). The disciples are to take their stand against the powers of darkness and drive evil out (Matt 10:1). They must be ready for the consequence of taking public stands because they will be brought before religious authorities (Sanhedrin and synagogue), governors, and kings (Matt 10:17). Jesus picked out the twelve and sent them out on mission. Mark says that Jesus asked them to go out two by two and together to take their stand against the powers of evil, to ask people to live in new ways, and to heal suffering (Mark 6:7–12). The disciples, in a word, imitate Jesus who was a great gatherer of people, all of whom would be missioned as well as gathered. The Spirit who led Jesus into his public life (Luke 4:14) is the same Spirit who guides the disciples and tells them what to say when the going gets rough (Matt 10:20). Matthew's final word is a sending into the whole world with the good news (Matt 28:16–20)—the great commission.

Paul develops the image of Christ the gatherer into a Christology in his First Letter to the Corinthians. It is the task of Jesus to gather all people into one family with Christ as head and then to bring that community of saints as well as himself as a gift

to God (1 Cor 15:20–28). The building up of community is important to Paul precisely because it is a Christological activity.
Gathered and being gathered, sending and being sent, are at the
core of our discipleship.

Sociological Insight into Being Gathered and Sent

At the center of our conceptual analysis of small faith communities is the recognition that they are what Evelyn and James
Whitehead have called intermediate (or "hybrid") social forms
(1992, 19–20). Small Christian communities are like what sociologists call "primary groups" (e.g., families) in that they are characterized by an emphasis on acceptance, loyalty, and close personal
relationships. But they are also like what sociologists call "task
groups" (e.g., teams in the workplace) in that they have a work to
perform. A proper concern for how they are gathered—for the
capacity of their members to communicate mutually, seek consensus, and utilize conflict creatively—is one of the hallmarks of
authentic SCCs. The other is due regard for how they are sent—for
the capacity of the community to join with others in seeking the
well-being of the larger social world to which they belong. In our
view the motivating heart of SCCs is their commitment to sustain
both an inner and a public conversation, to be like a family and like
a task group simultaneously. The purpose of this chapter is to lay
out the dimensions of that challenging, double-edged vocation.

The Two Basic Dimensions
of Small Christian Communities

The distinction between the primary ("gathered") and task
("sent") dimensions of SCCs is analogous to the difference between
psychological and sociological understandings of community. We will
introduce each of these in turn. In his classic work on community-
based approaches to mental health, psychologist Seymour Sarason
offers a magnificent description of the "psychological sense of community" (1974, 157):

Precisely because we all experience the presence or
absence of a psychological sense of community, however

restricted it may be in terms of the size of the referent group, its characteristics are not hard to state. The perception of similarity to others, an acknowledged interdependence with others, a willingness to maintain this interdependence by giving to or doing for others what one expects from them, the feeling that one is part of a larger dependable and stable structure—these are the ingredients of the psychological sense of community. You know when you have it and when you don't. It is not without conflict or changes in its strength. It is at its height when the existence of the referent group is challenged by external events…; it is also at its height…in times of celebration.…It is one of the major bases for self-definition and the judging of external events. The psychological sense of community is not a mystery to the person who experiences it. It is a mystery to those who do not experience it but hunger for it.

Here we view the phenomenon of community from the inside out, as it were. Sarason's description emphasizes what community feels like and entails subjectively. Small communities must gather in mutuality. This is the "primary group" aspect of small faith communities. It corresponds to what we shall call their "inner" (gathered) life, which is the focus of chapter 5.

The other side of a small community's life is its engagement in the larger social world of which it is a part. The understanding that the church does not exist in isolation for itself alone but rather in and for the world is deeply embedded in the historic Jewish and Christian traditions. The classic expression of this aspect of biblical faith is to be found in the voices of the Jewish prophets. In *The Prophetic Imagination*, Walter Brueggemann offers the following account of the public vocation of people of faith (1978, 22):

Surely history consists primarily in speaking and being answered, in crying and being heard. If that is true it means that there can be no history in the empire because the cries are never heard and the speaking is never answered. And if the task of prophecy is to empower people to engage in history, then it means evoking cries that expect answers, learning to address them where they will be taken seriously, and ceasing to look to the numbed and dull empire that never intended to answer in the first place.

Here the faith community is looked at from the outside, so to speak, from the perspective of its mission to engage in history, to make its presence felt in the current "empire" of economics and politics. Small communities must be sent prophetically. This is the "task group" aspect of small faith communities. It corresponds to what we shall call their "public" (sent) life, which is the focus of chapter 6.

We want to declare our firm conviction that both of these dimensions are integral to the biblical character of small faith communities. A "small community of faith" with a strong inner life but no viable public presence is in truth a support group; a "small Christian community" with notable public impact but little development of its inner life is in truth a social-action group. We will argue both on biblical grounds and in light of our own experience and research that to claim authentically the title "community of faith" means to accept the challenge of developing and integrating an inner and a public dimension. To participate in an SCC is a complex and challenging process largely because it demands of its members high levels of *both* relationship and task orientations if it is to work. A faithful, vibrant small community will provide a strong psychological sense of belonging for its members, even as it will learn how to address hard and timely questions regarding justice and mercy to the powers that be. And it will discover that, far from operating at each other's expense, the inner and public dimensions, when held in creative tension, deepen and enrich each other. In fact we suggest that balancing and rebalancing these two concerns in the real world in which a community finds itself, using the guidance of biblical vision, *is* the life of a small community of faith. Small faith communities are gathered and sent.

The use of sociological categories helps us interpret many of the challenges of Christian discipleship. We are more than "a hybrid group with primary and secondary characteristics," but neither are we ever less than that. Grace has many names.

Small Christian Communities as Intentional

The communities we described in the previous chapters are made up of Christians who have deliberately chosen to cast their lots with other Christians. This deliberate choice makes them intentional communities rather than simply spontaneous or random gatherings. Despite our legendary cultural loneliness, it is not easy for Western individualists to cast our lot significantly with anyone outside our primary groups. Intentional community is not "natural" for us.

"Intentional" means "deliberate" or "consciously chosen." This word is our way of highlighting the fact that within the relatively affluent contemporary culture of the West, large numbers of persons will ordinarily not be drawn into small communities out of necessity, as has been the case in Latin America. The worldwide movement of small Christian communities can be authentically appropriated in and for Western culture only in a voluntary and democratic fashion. It is a way of life to which persons must be invited. The kind of community life which we are about to describe in detail cannot and should never be forced on anyone. It must be chosen intentionally.

We want to present a working model of small Christian communities. We call it a "working model" because it is intended as a practical tool for reflection and action. Let's begin with a definition. A small Christian community is a relatively small group of persons committed to ongoing conversation and shared action along four distinguishable but interrelated dimensions:

- They are consistently committed to a high degree of mutuality in the relationships among them.
- They pursue an informed critical awareness of and an active engagement within the cultural, political, and economic realities of their society.
- They cultivate and sustain a network of empowering connections with other persons, communities, and movements of similar purpose.
- They attend faithfully to the Christian character of their community's life.

We have just named the four core dimensions of an SCC in contemporary language. Terms like "mutuality," "network," and "empowering" are drawn from our contemporary vocabulary. But such terms can also be translations, attempts to revivify the ideals of our ancient Christian story in the everyday life of our time, to help us name and envision a form of Christian praxis in and for our today.

"Mutuality," for instance, is a way of naming the *koinonia*, the belonging and equality, the solidarity among persons characteristic of authentic Christian existence. As we saw in chapter 3, *koinonia* pertains to relationships *within* particular small communities as well as to relationships *among* various small communities. As we learn to participate in face-to-face relationships of mutuality, we are actually nurturing *koinonia* among us. As we learn to network effectively with others of common purpose, we are extending and deepening the web of *koinonia*—of belonging and equality—which our Christian story holds to be sacred.

"Pursuing an informed critical awareness of and an active engagement within the cultural, political, and economic realities of our lives" is simply a contemporary way of naming a form of the *diakonia*, the caring service, to which authentic Christian existence calls us. "Private" Christianity is a profound contradiction of our ancient tradition. Faith is never just "between me and God." Our Christian vocation is radically social or relational. When we learn to reflect together theologically in a constructively critical fashion and to engage actively with the world around us in the light of such reflection, we are extending our *diakonia*—our caring and serving presence—into the contemporary world. This extension is not elective; it is our biblical obligation.

Finally, "to attend faithfully to the Christian character of our community's life" is to keep the Christian *kerygma* with its dangerous memories and transformative hopes at the center of our collective consciousness (and unconsciousness), and to celebrate that memory and hope together in the sacramental moments of Christian *leitourgia*. In rituals of word and sacrament, members of SCCs keep their personal and collective moods and motivations attuned to the challenging and consoling contours of their sacred story. In so doing, they place the everyday acts of their interaction with one another and the surrounding world in the ultimate context of the sacred Christian narratives of justice and love.

Therefore, to say that SCCs are characterized by mutuality, social engagement, networking, and Christian remembrance is to say that these small groups are concretely involved together in the genuine praxis of *koinonia, diakonia, kerygma* and *leitourgia*. It is to say that they are truly ecclesial units, truly church. Many human groups are characterized by one or several of these four attributes; an SCC is the social form that it is because it intends to strive toward the faithful embodiment of all of them simultaneously.

Practical Theology: Reflection and Action in Small Christian Communities

A special form of conversation requiring both reflection and action and wonderfully suited to SCCs is often named "practical theology." This expression has a comfortable ring to the ears of most Americans, known as they are throughout the world for their no-nonsense, down-to-earth attitudes. But our usual associations with the word "practical"—that is, "useful" or "applicable" or "relevant to everyday concerns—are misleading in this instance. In order to eliminate the confusion, the method could have been entitled "Theology of Praxis," but that would only have substituted one kind of ambiguity for another.

Practical theology names a cluster of methods for doing theology. What those varying methods have in common is the insistence that the point of theological interpretation is not simply to contemplate or comprehend the world as it is, but to contribute to the world's becoming what God intends it to be, as that intention has been interpreted by the great theistic traditions. Now the view that theology has a concrete contribution to make to the actual world might seem like common sense, but our Christian religious instincts have long been primarily formed by the perspective of classical theism, namely, that religious interpretation is about the "beatific vision," knowing or contemplating the essence of God. The title practical theology signals the intention to stress the faith's vocation to affect history.

The version of practical theology which we will outline here is our revision of the "revised correlational method" proposed by theologian David Tracy in *Blessed Rage for Order* (1979), which in turn is a reworking of the correlational theological method developed by

Paul Tillich. Such methods are called "correlational" because they work by holding two things in reciprocal relationship—our religious traditions and the state of the actual world in which we live. In our revision of Tracy's model for practical theology, the critical conversation between faith and culture, which every Christian community must continuously undertake, always has a concrete objective in action, namely, the transformation of persons, societies, and cultures so that our treatment of each other and the earth brings peace. Our version of practical theology, in other words, involves not only our critical intelligence but also our capacity for committed and effective action. The practical theological method outlined below has been developed by the authors in collaboration with other members of the faculty of the Institute for Ministry of Loyola University New Orleans.

Practical theology requires that members of SCCs intentionally interpret their social and cultural situation. This process begins by prayerfully considering the world as it is, lifting up an aspect of it which particularly concerns us, and articulating the nature of our concern including our "gut" reactions to it. The word "concern" here carries the meaning developed in the Quaker tradition, that is, of having one's attention called to an aspect of reality by God. The Quaker understanding of concern is very much like the meaning associated with the term "burden" in African-American churches. When a black pastor says that "God has placed a burden on my heart for public-housing residents," he or she means that God is directing them to pay special attention to the people who live in those circumstances.

Through their membership in a broad-based community organization (which we will discuss in chapter 6), small communities of faith in New Orleans first identified and are now pursuing their concerns for the well-being of the larger community in the areas of public education, child care, affordable home ownership, and living-wage jobs. To which initiative a particular community commits itself depends upon its discernment of its primary concerns and available resources.

Having identified a concern, an SCC must subject it to appropriate critical scrutiny, lest it become caught up in the "concern du jour" mentality so pervasive in our culture, in which pressing situations of need get their fifteen minutes of attention in the public eye and are then forgotten, with no serious long-term commitment. Having submitted its concern to critical reflection, the SCC must then undertake a disciplined, practical investigation of what is causing the situation, with a view to understanding it well enough to affect it positively. In doing so, the group is not seeking the knowledge of the expert, but something beyond what "everybody knows" about the concern. We call this range of knowing, which lies between expertise and common sense, "practical wisdom" or "working knowledge." It is the kind of knowledge which makes one a good parent, principal, minister, or community leader, a knowledge which lets one make the best of real situations. Practical wisdom leads not only to the accomplishment of necessary tasks, but also to the empowerment of those involved.

For example, through participation in their community organization's working group on public education, SCC members in New Orleans have begun to develop a working knowledge of the dilemmas facing public schools in a racially divided urban environment. They have discovered, for example, that the Louisiana state constitution provides that owners of homes assessed at less than $75,000 in value shall pay no real-estate tax. Property taxes are a major source of financial support for public schools in most communities in the U.S. So under Louisiana's current constitution, areas in which schools are likeliest to be needy are also the areas likeliest to be exempt from taxes. Those who want to increase the level of financial support for the New Orleans public schools must either seek an amendment to the state constitution or create another source of public financial support for community schools.

When SCC members have developed a practical understanding of some aspect of their concern, they then prayerfully select an aspect of our faith tradition—scriptural text, theological classic, church teaching, and so on—which seems relevant to it for an initial reading and response, including their "gut" reactions to what they've chosen. Then they undertake a historically informed exegesis of that material so as to come to a deeper understanding of its significance, one that moves beyond initial impressions and responses toward a fuller appreciation of that which is being interpreted. Such disciplined interpretation requires that members attend to the historical circumstances which gave rise to the chosen text (the "world behind the text"), the form and content of the text as they have received it (the "world in the text"), and the possibilities for transformed living which the text provokes them to consider (the "world in front of the text").

In response to the vision of a key African-American pastor, SCC members belonging to a broad-based community organization in New Orleans have reflected upon, studied, and taken to heart in a very special way the twenty-ninth chapter of the book of Jeremiah. That text is a letter which the prophet sent from Jerusalem to his people just exiled to Babylon at the end of the sixth century B.C.E. The seventh verse of that chapter takes the form of a remarkable admonition: "But seek the peace of the city where I have sent you into exile, and pray to the Lord on its behalf, for in its peace you will find your peace." The SCCs of metropolitan New Orleans have been repeatedly accosted by that text and are attempting to fashion a public life which is both feasible and faithful in light of it.

SCC members do not need the expertise of the scripture scholar or academic theologian, but they do need more than an uncritically received, taken-for-granted understanding of our tradition. A practical knowledge of our faith tradition lets us interpret accurately what it really had to say to a community of our ancestors in faith; it also lets us be aware of the faith tradition's distortions by the "-isms"—sexism, ethnocentrism, classism, or anthropocentrism. Only such a disciplined process of shared interpretation allows a community of faith to be properly appreciative and critical of what their tradition's classic symbols, texts, events, and persons have to say here and now.

Having interpreted both their situation and tradition with care, members of SCCs must then discern their contemporary obligations as people of faith in today's world and decide how to act accordingly. In doing so they must prayerfully consider what would constitute feasible and faithful responses and make a choice from the available possibilities. A feasible response is simply one that is possible for this community in the world as it is; a faithful response is one which rings true to the religious tradition they take as their guide. To paraphrase Edward Schillebeeckx, feasibility without faithfulness is barbarism, and faithfulness without feasibility is superstition.

Through the process of discernment outlined above, some of the New Orleans SCCs have joined the task force at work on public education while others have focused on providing access to affordable child care for persons of moderate to low income.

Having made a choice for a particular course of action, SCC members must then plan an adequately detailed intervention based on that choice, implement it carefully, and rigorously evaluate both what practical difference the action made in addressing their concern and its religious adequacy from the standpoint of their tradition. Finally the community opens itself to its world anew and makes itself receptive to that to which God will call its attention next.

In collaboration with members of larger congregations in an effort which crosses lines of race, religion, and economic status, New Orleans SCCs are currently involved in careful ongoing analysis of the realities surrounding public education and child care in their metropolitan area. This analysis has led so far, to give one example, to the initial implementation of a strategy for rebuilding the base of adult support necessary for a successful school. This is being done in seven carefully selected public schools by reaching out to principals, teachers, staff, parents, and other concerned adults in the wider community.

So this is what we mean by "doing practical theology" in SCCs: attending carefully with our heads and hearts both to the world as it is and to the world as our faith traditions teach us it should be, asking "What must we do?" in the light of that attention, doing it, and then evaluating what we have done. This disciplined rhythm of reflection-action-reflection by members of SCCs *is* practical theology. It is at the center of the vocation to which members of communities of faith are called. In engaging the world and their faith tradition through practical theology, members of SCCs are continually challenged to recognize that a poorly understood world is as much a disaster as a poorly understood Word.

At the risk of overstating a point, we want to emphasize once again what we mean by "reading" our faith tradition and our world. These are indeed complex realities, scholars devote their entire lives to relatively small facets of them. For example, a religious scholar may be an expert on John's gospel, while a secular expert may focus on just public transportation. This kind of specialized expertise is not required for SCCs. The point is not that SCC members become urban sociologists or scripture scholars, but rather that their practical abilities to read their world and their

tradition—and to empower others to do so—are enhanced by serious study of the work of experts. Christian discipleship, ministry,
and leadership must be informed by the work of experts, but should
not be dominated by it. Our point might be put in this way: Experts
have their place in the work of practical theology and must be kept
in their place! Responsibility for theological reflection leading to
committed action rests finally with members of local communities
of faith.

It is our conviction that a method of practical theological
reflection needs to be incorporated into SCC rituals. Practical theology is a flexible and forgiving method. It can be broken into parts
which are engaged in successive meetings, or worked through in a
single session of two to three hours. It allows SCC members to
return to previous steps and rework them in the light of new information or changing circumstances. As members experiment with a
form of practical theology suitable for their SCC, they should
remember that the underlying purpose of practical theological
reflection is to sustain a disciplined conversation between their faith
community's vision of the world as it should be and the often harsh
realities of the world as it is, a conversation that leads to faithful and
feasible action.

The Social Ecology of
Intentional Christian Communities

Small Christian communities exist as ecclesial units within a
complex social web. "Ecology" is our contemporary name for the
study of relationships between organisms and their environment.
We are coming to realize that the ecology of all life is systemic in
character, that what happens and fails to happen in our world for
good and ill is a matter of relationships and their effects on everything and everyone concerned. No aspect of life can be adequately
understood apart from a profound awareness of its context. Human
beings are slowly but surely arriving at an awareness of our natural
and social ecological web; we are developing the capacity to live in
a systems world. Christian communities can simply not afford to
ignore their embeddedness within this web of systems.

Members of Christian communities begin to appreciate the
relational character of our world when we recognize that anyone's

"individual" becoming really refers to how she or he is emerging from the particular contexts—planetary, familial, social, economic, political, and cultural—of life. The futures which we might create together are, for better and for worse, in continuity with the history of events within the complex webs of relationship just named. We are always already situated within a particular world with a concrete history; the futures we might create will always bear the mark of our context and its history. One pertinent example of this insight for our purposes here is that, like dioceses and parishes, the contemporary movement of SCCs is situated within and emerging from the history of the larger church of which it is a part.

To live responsibly in a relational world is to have one's life profoundly shaped by the awareness that existence is an individual matter only to a limited extent. It is to realize that, like it or not, we are all in this together. To paraphrase Teilhard de Chardin, our past is not part of history possessed by us totally, but rather all of history possessed by us partially. By the same token our future is not an isolated piece of what might be, which we own autonomously as if it were our private property; it is part of the common possible future of our species nested within the universe's possible futures. Something analogous might obviously be said about the reality of SCCs today in relationship to the larger church. They are not the sole possessors of their own piece of church, but rather all of church history is reflected in their unique character. Their possible futures are of a piece with the church's possibilities.

It is illuminating for members of Christian communities to understand our world as a complex relational web. The principal public commitments of SCCs—the full inclusion of people of color, women, and other formerly "invisibles" within society; peace; economic and social justice worldwide; and intercultural communication and respect—cannot be adequately understood and addressed apart from a practical and systematic analysis of human society and history. In order to foster that kind of understanding for members of Christian communities, we will present a brief overview of the web of relationships within which everyday lives are played out and then use that overview in order to situate the particular social form called community.

This model is conceptualized as structured in three levels: microsocial, macrosocial, and mediating structures. Like all models it is a simplification. In order to be useful it should be complex enough to capture the interrelatedness of the social world that is the real context in which Christian communities must survive and thrive, and simple enough to support reflective action by community members.

Microsocial Structures

"Microsocial" structures are the small, immediate groups of our everyday lives, for example, families or other living groups, work teams, support groups, citizen boards, classrooms, and certain voluntary associations. In contemporary Western society, most of our time is spent interacting in a complex variety of such settings. The quality of these relationships obviously has an enormous effect on people's sense of well-being and quality of life. According to this definition, small communities of faith are microsocial groups.

The structure and dynamics of any small face-to-face group constitute a kind of dance in which the participants have interlocking and reciprocal roles. The effects of this dance on individual participants are indeed profound. As contemporary family-systems theories have made clear, no person in a group is an island, immune or cut off from the system's effects. Interpersonal events in microsystems are in important ways a matter of internalizing a system's repeating pattern of interpersonal events. We revisit this issue in depth in chapter 5.

The extent and lasting effects of our interdependence within important groups at the microsocial level are further revealed when we recognize that typical patterns of behavior and emotion are not merely ways that people cope while they are members of a particular system, which can then be easily dropped when and if they leave it. The roles played in these groups constitute the social and emotional foundations of our individual personalities. Family groups, for example, provide our basic training for personhood. Microsocial groups are not just places where autonomous individuals hang around playing certain roles for a while; they are the places where we experience the web of relationships face to face, and that entire web is the source of the selves we are becoming.

It is important to be aware of the networks of microsocial groups in our lives. Thinking this way can help us to remember that we are not just a family member and then later a participant on a work team and still later a participant in a faith-sharing group; rather, we belong to a set of microsystems simultaneously. The pattern of reciprocal effects among our microsocial groups constitutes another aspect of the overall relational context within which Christian communities arise. What happens in our household has profound effects on our participation in the workplace and vice versa. Indeed, one of the most common complaints of contemporary people is that there is never enough time and energy for adequate participation in our network of microsocial roles—we are chronically torn between and among our roles.

Like individual persons within a group, individual groups within microsocial networks affect and are affected by each other. Together they constitute a system of their own, a complex and recurring pattern of mutually influential interaction within which our personal development is always unfolding. Sociologically speaking, SCCs are part of that system. Our network of face-to-face groups is like a smaller web within a larger one. This larger web we call the "macrosocial" structures.

Macrosocial Structures

The term "macrosocial" refers to those large institutions and organizations which, while not immediately present to us in everyday life deeply affect our existence, like the IRS, the New York Stock Exchange, the Roman Catholic Church, and so on. The institutions and organizations of government, the economy, mass media, religion, and education have profound and continuous effects on events at the micro-level. The smaller and more personal systems can and do affect macrosocial structures, though we typically and understandably experience the influence as running primarily in the other direction. In the next section of this chapter we will begin to consider how microsystems like SCCs might affect macro-systems; we'll continue that exploration in more depth and specificity in chapter 5 on the public life of small communities. For now, let's concentrate on the influence of larger structures on smaller ones.

The microsystems of U.S. society, including small Christian communities, are situated today within the larger socioeconomic context called an "advanced industrial society." Such a society is one which has undergone two important transformations in its basic economic structure. The first is a shift of the majority of workers from agriculture to various industries. The second, which continues rapidly in American society, is the movement of a significant number of workers from industrial to service occupations. Thus an advanced industrial society is one in which a large proportion of the labor force is employed in retailing, health, education, government, and other fields. Such a society requires an incredibly intricate network of production, distribution, transportation, communication, government, and legal systems. This interlocking network of large, influential institutions and organizations is one aspect of the macrosocial dimension of the web of relationships.

Advanced industrial societies did not appear in the world full blown; they evolved over the course of human history. As a result of macrosocial changes, the role of micro-level groups like the family has undergone significant transformations. These transformations speak to us about the importance of megasystem events for the life of small Christian communities.

Until quite recently the economic division of labor in advanced industrial society (a macrosocial reality) tended to send males out into the world outside the home to provide the material resources necessary for their families' survival. It likewise tended to keep females at work inside the home, providing the social and emotional resources required by their families. Most men and women in such a society didn't experience a clear moment of personal choice about whether to go out into the marketplace or work at home; it was a matter of fitting into the economic realities, the macrosocial norms of their time.

These norms fostered the economic dependency of women, who were expected to take up their economic roles within the home. Thus many of the educational and on-the-job experiences that allowed men to pursue economic security outside the home were systematically denied to women. When a woman has been outside the employment mainstream for a significant period of time, it is difficult if not impossible for her to move outside the home and make a living adequate to support a family. For similar reasons, she probably has no version of a pension plan or other form of the economic security that her husband has been steadily accruing over the years by virtue of his employment outside the home. As a consequence, she typically faces bleak economic prospects on her own.

The very bleakness of these prospects kept (and still keep) women in marital relationships where they are victims of various kinds of abuse. We now know clearly that marital relationships characterized by such desperate dependency and abuse predispose resulting children to the same dependent and abusive patterns of relationship, not just during their childhoods but in their adult lives as well. Clearly such a macroeconomic situation is in no sense a result of the personal decisions of individuals; it is its own reality, with complex social and historical causes. This example illustrates the power of large systems over the course of individual lives and the functioning of groups at the microsocial level.

Macrosocial structures exert powerful formative effects on the functioning of all other levels of society and, therefore, on the development of all persons. Its functioning is likewise affected by them. Macrostructures do not unilaterally determine events, but their effects are felt always and everywhere. Small Christian communities are of course not exempt from these effects.

Another macro-dimension refers not to particular groups, organizations, or institutions, but rather to the culture that is always forming and being formed by them. Culture itself affects and is affected by the ways that the other social levels take shape. Culture is an inherited set of understandings and practices which organize a people's life. It is a world of shared meanings carried and transmitted in symbols, especially language. As persons become acculturated, which always happens within the web of systems just described, they learn to experience and to understand their worlds in specific ways. They come to take for granted a particular assumptive world or map of reality.

Culture lends its shape to and is shaped by the structure and dynamics of both our small, face-to-face groups and the large institutions and organizations just described. The pattern of events within the whole systemic web of our lives emerges from complex, multidirectional interactions between the micro- and macro-levels. No level dictates events at other levels, but only influences them, albeit sometimes so profoundly as to appear almost as a determining force. Members of intentional Christian communities are certainly affected by realities in the web of macrosocial relations in which they live, such as the myriad ways in which pressures to achieve and consume are brought to bear on themselves and their children through advertising and peer pressure. They may affect those events as well. The capacity of small communities to exercise such transformative effects, to have a potent public life, depends on their ability to join with others in mediating structures.

Mediating Structures

As we have seen, persons, groups, organizations, and institutions exist within a complex pattern of influences. While by no means always symmetrical or equal in their effects, these interactions are always reciprocal: Every person, group, organization, and institution is affected for better and for worse by participation within the web of relationships, while having their own effects on that web. We live within a relational world of reciprocal influences. No vital, sustainable movement of SCCs is possible unless its relationship to the web of relationships at both micro- and macro-levels is carefully taken into account. Even then it won't be easy!

People routinely move back and forth between smaller and more personal microsocial groups and the larger and impersonal macrosocial systems. Because these larger systems are so often alienating and depersonalizing in their effects, the citizens of complex advanced industrial societies often feel no choice but to seek meaning and participation within smaller, face-to-face groups. Because we so often feel relatively helpless about such things as racism, inflation, consumerism, and foreign policy, we understandably tend to leave them to others and to turn to family, friendship groups, and community for acknowledgement and feelings of efficacy.

But there is a twofold problem with this common and understandable strategy for coping with events in the contemporary world. First, it tends to alienate us further from the larger systems that have so much effect on us. As a consequence, our political and economic order—the bedrock of any social world—can lose legitimacy in the hearts and minds of more and more of its participants. This heightens the temptation to abdicate our proper roles as bona fide participants in the institutions of government, economy, institutional church, and culture—to leave the guidance of all of that in "their" hands. In our absence these macrostructures go right on having massively important effects on everyone's lives. So genuinely democratic public order among us becomes more and more difficult to sustain.

Second, the capacity of microstructures like the family to carry the entire weight of personal meaning and involvement is actually quite limited. How can families, friendship groups, or small communities possibly counterbalance the massive alienating effects of society and culture on the large scale? Clearly they cannot do so alone. In fact, as current debates on welfare and medical care in Western society illustrate, politics and the economy have major effects on what is likely to occur within microsocial groups. Events at the micro-level of society are so often at the mercy of events at the macro-level that it often seems that the smaller and more personal systems of our lives can only offer us a kind of "haven in a heartless world." The increasing fragility and vulnerability of these havens is, however, more and more apparent.

If SCCs are to be more than islands of belonging and support for their members, to have more than an inner life, they must develop their capacity to connect with other groups and institutions around common concerns and interests.

The power of cultural and religious groups and of local, politically-attuned voluntary associations to affect the life chances of their members was nowhere more powerfully evidenced than in the civil rights movement in the United States. African-American church leaders and leaders of other local associations coalesced into a formidable collective agent of social transformation and liberation for their people. The improved life chances for people of color resulting from the struggle for civil rights are directly attributable to the social bonds which gave meaning and purpose to those engaged in that struggle; the African-American church was the primary locus of those empowering bonds.

The web of relationships within which we exist is constituted not only by economic layers and political institutions (macrosocial structures) and small, face-to-face settings (microsocial structures) but also by the cultural groups to which we belong, the congregations with which we are affiliated, the neighborhood organizations in which we participate, and a myriad of other forms of voluntary association. The pattern of these affiliations, which sociologists call "mediating structures," contributes to our location within a social world. To "mediate" is to be in the middle, linking two other things. Mediating structures have the power to give microsocial groups like families and small communities a voice and some power in the arena of macrosocial structures. As the example of the civil rights movement clearly indicates, a well-organized web of mediating structures—congregations, neighborhood organizations, civic associations—can indeed move macrosocial mountains. Chapter 6 of this book will show how understanding the logic of mediating structures allows intentional faith communities to be creatively and prophetically engaged with the larger social systems which shape our lives so profoundly.

Closing

Pressing, often overwhelming, sometimes demoralizing dilemmas face people in our time—issues, for example, of economic and social justice for African Americans, women, and other marginalized groups. The hyper-individualism of Western culture makes solidarity with other persons a dilemma. Given the huge, intricate web of institutions and organizations of advanced industrial societies, the possibility of participating in a group where belonging is experienced through mutual relationships, where society and history are engaged and not retreated from, and where the centuries-old conversation called Christian tradition is faithfully and ritually celebrated in and for our time touches the deepest longings of many people.

This is indeed the claim and promise of small Christian communities. It is a claim not in the sense of ownership, but rather in the sense of a piece of earth to be worked painstakingly and with fidelity. And it is a promise not in the sense of a guarantee, but rather in the sense of a possibility which might unfold into concrete actuality. The social form we are calling small Christian community does indeed hold the potential for deeply creative interaction with other individuals (inner life) as well as with the larger cultural, political, and economic structures of our world (public life). But this creativity will emerge in society and history in a sustainable way only if small Christian communities intentionally stake their claims and keep their promises in their specific social location and in fidelity to the sacred stories of their tradition.

At one level, an intentional commitment to Christian community is a promise to stay engaged over time with a particular group of persons in the four tasks described above. Such a promise gives the community a special right to our time, energy, and care. But at a deeper level, commitment makes our very *selves* available to specific others in a privileged way. Something of our cherished privacy and individuality is always given up in authentic commitment to community. This is in fact one of the major uphill struggles facing a movement of these communities in a country such as the U.S., with its profoundly individualistic and autonomous world view and ethos. On the other hand, the distress that many Americans feel in our collective "pursuit of loneliness" is a powerful cultural incentive to a new form of belonging.

Beyond granting a particular group of persons privileged access to our selves, a commitment to community is an acknowledgment of the fact that "being related" is central to human existence. It is a way not merely of coping with, but even of celebrating, life as participation in a complex and diverse world of relationships. What we acknowledge in committing ourselves to intentional community is that our individual and collective identities do not exist prior to our relatings, but arise out of them. Our sense of identity—as individuals, Christians, Americans, and so on—emerges from and is continually being transformed within our concrete web of connections to life.

Commitment to the shared life and work of a small community is a recognition of the relational character of human life. Commitment to the shared life and work of a small *Christian* community is an acknowledgement of the sacred character of our relationships. Christians in small communities are attempting to allow the relational character of their sacred narrative to shape their existence profoundly. At the center of the dangerously liberating memory which is Christian tradition is a communitarian or relational vision of human life in the world. In such a vision my life is never just about me, it is always about us as well. We matter and we affect each other, all of us, living and dead.

We have said that commitment to a small Christian community entails a promise over time. There are many worthwhile experiences that can happen in an hour or a weekend or a month; intentional community is not one of them. There is an issue of continuity here, of the staying power of our claims and promises. It has been observed that when an intimate relationship is working well there is a strong tendency for persons to commit and recommit themselves to it, as if there is a natural strain toward permanence in creative, intimate relationships. In our experience an analogous point can be made as regards creative community dynamics—they naturally incline members toward commitment and recommitment.

The promise that is commitment to an SCC is generated and regenerated in the everyday acts of community life: having mutual conversation, collectively engaging the world, standing in common cause with others of similar purpose, and possessing shared experiences of Christian memory and anticipation in word and sacrament; that is to say, in our shared praxis of *koinonia, diakonia, kerygma* and *leitourgia*. In sustaining an inner and a public life in everyday acts over time, we come to feel the efficacy of intentionally belonging to an SCC flowing into and out of us. The disciplining, liberating conversation that is community has begun our conversion. The body of Christ, gathered in particular times and places, is sent to seek the city's peace.

5

Internal Mission:
Consensus, Conflict, and Leadership
in Small Church Communities

Introduction

The two scripture passages that have most captured the Christian imagination are both from John. The first is that the Word was made flesh and pitched his tent among us. The second is that God is love. In its own way, each is full of incredible requirement as well as incredible consolation. Each forces the worldly shape of God's presence and the worldly shape of God's love upon our sensibilities. One cannot take leave of the world, of historical experience, to find God. One cannot take leave of loving one's sisters and brothers to love God alone. Whoever claims to love God but meanwhile hates another person is a liar, says John. Whoever backs away from the difficult areas of human love backs away from the difficult areas of loving God. John didn't write those words, but he might have. In love we have to keep "showing up" whether we feel like it or not, and often we don't. Remembered moments of ecstasy call us "there." Our ecstasies are not random high moments. They come as unplanned, uncontrived gift, as sudden flower—but only when the relational earth has been tilled and cared for. This chapter is about tilling relational earth in a garden called small Christian community, where our love for each other and our love for God are flowers on the same stem. The concrete demands of turning over relational earth, tilling it, are daunting, but there's no flowering without it. That's why conversation and conversion are connected. We hope to place our contemporary interpretation of communication at the disposal of our understanding of the body of Christ and vice versa.

The glue that holds any web of relationships together is communication. In fact researchers have established the fact that human beings in each other's presence cannot *not* communicate! But when boundaries are not clear and people become over involved in each other's lives, relationship becomes fusion and growth is stifled. It is equally true that when interaction remains politely superficial there is no real connection and consequently no vitality in interpersonal life. Creative relationship makes its appearance in the space between fusion and isolation.

Small communities of faith are not exempt from the principles which govern all interpersonal communication. In this chapter we explore the role of face-to-face interaction in SCCs, for the pulsing heart of a small community is its communicative interaction. The quality of communal existence can be no better than the quality of conversation which constitutes it. That is as true of our conversation with God as of our conversation with each other. The quality of both inner ("gathered") and public ("sent") dimensions of a small community's life depends upon the adequacy and depth of communication among community members. There is no preexisting blueprint for creating these two basic dimensions within an SCC. Taking joint responsibility and holding one another accountable for that creative work is precisely what community membership entails. An inner and a public life emerge only through sustained, creative conversation within the community.

Biblical Perspectives on Consensus, Conflict, and Leadership

For members of small Christian communities, being with one another is more than merely a pragmatic concern about good communication as a means to another end. How we are together in the world with other persons is for Christians also a matter of religious significance. Members of SCCs are challenged by an authentic reading of their own sacred texts to take relationships in community life with ultimate seriousness.

The account of communication and decision making in SCCs which follows here is a modern-language version of the ancient awareness that relationships must embody certain qualities if they are to bear good fruit. Chief among these qualities is equal respect and care for one's own experience and that of others. To comport ourselves with such respect in our everyday communication is to engage in mutual conversation. It is one crucial expression of loving our neighbors as we love ourselves. The authentic religious heritage of Judaism and Christianity is a communal and not an individualistic one. It shows how we are to be together in the world, not just how we are to be as good individuals. It reminds us that "Who is my neighbor?" is our most fundamental kind of question. For Jews and Christians such love is also at the same time the primary symbol of our covenantal relationship with a God who loves us.

As we have already stressed, people must engage in a certain quality of conversation if the reality called community is to emerge among them in vital form—if, in the ancient Pauline language of our tradition, they are to become "one body in Christ and members of one another." When Paul offers directives about the truth that must characterize relationships—about handling anger and grudges, about using a certain kind of language in speaking to one another, about being gentle and patient—he is not speaking only of good community dynamics in a pragmatic sense, but of "the way you have learned from Christ," of "the one Body and one Spirit," of "the peace that binds you together." He is speaking of ultimate realities. We become the people of God as we become one Body.

There is a crucial connection between the quality of interaction of "one bodyness"—in Christian community and the ongoing creative transformation of community members and their world; this is one of the central assumptions of the biblical tradition. This strong Jewish and early Christian emphasis on the social or relational character of being human has been dangerously eroded in modern Western culture, with the American ethic of individualism being a case in point. This erosion is also apparent in the widespread modern "privatization" of religion ("The only important question is: Have I accepted Jesus Christ as my personal savior?"). Within the dominant culture of individualism, we have come to live as if we first exist and then form relationships in the pursuit of our interests.

The apostle who gave us the metaphor of the body of Christ was not an academician who prepared treatises. He was a brilliant pastoral theologian responding to specific issues in community. His theology welled up out of the encounter between his interpretation of the crucified and risen Christ and the specific issues of life in the communities he founded. Paul taught that if we are members of one another as the body of Christ, then we are mutually implicated in one another's lives. The Greek word for "one another" is *allelon*, and it occurs ninety-four times in the New Testament, about a third of them in Paul's letters. He uses the word to describe what is best about community when we honor one another, and what is worst in community when we dishonor one another. We can pick up the flavor by seeing just a few of these as examples. The word *allelon* occurs in each of the following.

> For I am longing to see you…so that we may be mutually encouraged by each other's faith, both yours and mine. (Rom 1:11–12)

> …love one another with mutual affection; outdo one another in showing honor. (Rom 12:10)

> So then, my brothers and sisters, when you come together to eat, wait for one another. (1 Cor 11:33)

> Greet one another with a holy kiss. (2 Cor 13:12)

When Paul hears of the self-centered behaviors of the Corinthian community at their gatherings for the Lord's Supper, he confronts them because they fail against *allelon*. He is not upset because they are being "impolite," but because they fail to recognize that being the body of Christ radically alters their relationships with one another. When Paul reprimands the community because they eat and drink "without discerning the body," he does not mean that they are failing to observe proper ritual rubrics, but rather that they have failed to recognize the body which they are. They have failed to connect their outside-of-the-Lord's-Supper behaviors with the meanings that are lodged inside it.

Because of our connection with one another, Paul pleads for agreement between us, that is, for all the consensus we can muster:

> If then there is any encouragement in Christ, any consolation from love, any sharing in the Spirit, any compassion and sympathy, make my job complete: be the same mind, having the same love, being in full accord and of

one mind....Let the same mind be in you that was in Christ Jesus. (Phil 2:1–2, 5)

For Paul the issue is almost ontological. One body can't have two minds! There has to be a singleness of spirit that animates us in our togetherness. At the practical level of daily living, and especially in communities that have a tight enough texture to recognize and address the exigencies of common life, genuine mutuality is a necessity. Skills at building consensus are not simply desirable, they are requisite. "May the God of steadfastness and encouragement grant you to live in harmony with one another, in accordance with Christ Jesus" (Rom 15:5).

Paul is, of course, aware that community also has to face up to "tough love," to borrow a contemporary phrase. He knew that dealing with conflict stemming from differences was part and parcel of membership in the body of Christ.

I myself feel confident about you, my brothers and sisters, that you yourselves are full of goodness, filled with knowledge, and able to instruct one another. (Rom 15:14)

But it is to Matthew that we look for sustained attention to conflict resolution.

In Matthew 6 Jesus instructs his followers on the nature of prayer in words that have come to be known as "The Lord's Prayer." One of the petitions is "forgive us our debts as we have forgiven those who are in debt to us." After the familiar prayer is completed, Matthew has Jesus underscore the reconciliation text:

For if you forgive others their trespasses, your heavenly Father will also forgive you; but if you do not forgive others, neither will your Father forgive your trespasses. (Matt 6:14–15)

This is an extraordinary teaching: Our reconciliation with God depends utterly on our reconciliation with each other. It gives rise to the requirement that Christian community be a place of reconciliation. Understanding that, any community will certainly be pressed to develop effective ways of handling conflict, and Matthew's narrative even outlines a specific process for doing so.

> If another member of the church sins against you, go and point out the fault when the two of you are alone. If the member listens to you, you have regained that one. But if you are not listened to, take one or two others along with you, so that every word may be confirmed by the evidence of two or three witnesses. If the member refuses to listen to them, tell it to the church; and if the offender refuses to listen even to the church, let such a one be to you as a Gentile and a tax collector. (Matt 18:15–17

Christian community cannot tolerate sustained failures of reconciliation.

And finally to the question of leadership. The biblical followers of Jesus form a discipleship of equals. Jesus teaches us the shape of the Kingdom:

> But you are not to be called rabbi, for you have one teacher, and you are all students. And call no one your father on earth, for you have one Father—the one in heaven. Nor are you to be called instructors, for you have one instructor, the Messiah. The greatest among you will be your servant. (Matt 23:8–11)

The key to Jesus' vision of relationship is that the parenthood of God makes all of us sisters and brothers. God's parenthood puts an end to human beings dominating each other. As Elisabeth Schüssler Fiorenza indicates, God's parenthood may not legitimately be used to support a form of domination like patriarchy because God's parenthood of all is a "critical subversion of all structures of domination" (Schüssler Fiorenza, 1983, 151). The theological and political dimensions of our lives are intimately related. Because we are children of the same God, we are called to be siblings; domination is not permissible within this community of equals.

As we noted in chapter 2, strange as it might seem, the most extraordinary legacy from our tradition regarding the exercise of leadership in the Christian community is not a particular form of organizational structure. Jesus made no prescriptions about that. Instead he gave us something much more significant—a metaphor.

Mark's Gospel recounts an argument on the road to Jerusalem, which for Mark is the road to the cross. James and John ask Jesus for a privileged place at his side in glory. The other ten followers are indignant with them. Jesus says to them:

> So Jesus called them and said to them, "You know that among the Gentiles those whom they recognize as their rulers lord it over them, and their great ones are tyrants over them. But it is not so among you; but whoever wishes to become great among you must be your servant, and whoever wishes to be first among you must be slave of all. For the Son of Man came not to be served but to serve, and to give his life a ransom for many." (Mark 10:42–45)

In Mark's Gospel, the disciples usually have a hard time understanding what Jesus is really saying (the women in Mark's story are more understanding and responsive). Matthew's version of the episode casts the disciples in a better light by having the mother of James and John ask for privileged places for her sons. Jesus' reply is the same.

A significant change takes place in Luke's version of this story. The argument about greatness occurs not on the road, but at the table of Jesus' final supper with his disciples, after the account of the institution of the Eucharist. Jesus repeats the answer he gave in Mark and Matthew's versions, but adds a meal metaphor.

> For who is greater, the one who is at the table or the one who serves? Is it not the one at the table? But I am among you as one who serves. (Luke 22:27)

Here again Jesus upends structures of domination. It is certainly for theological reasons that Luke takes this story off the road to Jerusalem and relocates it at the Last Supper. What could give a clearer message to a community celebrating Eucharist than to hear this discussion about leadership take place within the very context of Jesus instituting the Eucharist?

John's Gospel does not recount the furor caused by the request of James and John. Instead he narrates a dramatic scene in which Jesus washes the feet of those present for the Last Supper. By taking the servant's role of washing feet, Jesus uses actions, not words, to give a message about how power is to function in the Christian community.

The Christian tradition's precious, powerful, and paradoxical metaphor for leadership is the servant. For most readers of this book, the most common experience of being served is with waiters and waitresses. Remember that a metaphor is an image which is both like and not like something else. So Christian leadership is like and not like being a servant. It is like being a servant in requiring that those who lead do so to build up the community and its members, not themselves; it is not like being a servant in that those who lead must have input, share their vision, and take an active hand in shaping the community's life.

Leaders who serve receive effects as well as having them. Servant leadership is the Christian tradition's great metaphor for leadership as an exercise of relational, not unilateral, power. When we practice servant leadership in SCCs, we locate everyday acts of initiating and responding within the ultimate context of Christian memories and expectations. We are with our sisters and brothers as ones who serve one another.

As we noted in the introductory chapter, our word in this book for the kind of communication which makes individual members into one body is *conversation*. Conversation serves as the inclusive framework for the material in both earlier and later chapters in this book. As Paul reminds us, Christian communities can create a vital shared life only by seeking *consensus* among their members, by being of "one mind." So we treat consensus in this chapter as the first three critical instances of conversation within community life. As Matthew well understood, because people are different, authentic relationships inevitably entail a degree of *conflict*. Thus conflict is the second critical event of conversation to be treated here. All of the evangelists give us renditions of the servant metaphor as a model for *leadership* in the Christian community. The forms of conversation called consensus, conflict, and leadership are the beating heart of the inner life of SCCs, and the subject matter of this chapter.

Conversation

> Conversation is a game with some hard rules: say only
> what you mean; say it as accurately as you can; listen to
> and respect what the other says, however different or
> other; be willing to correct or defend opinions if chal-
> lenged by the conversation partner; be willing to argue if
> necessary, to confront if demanded, to endure necessary
> conflict, to change your mind if the evidence suggests it.
> (Tracy, 1987, 19)

> A precondition of friendly relationships was the system-
> atic avoidance of any topic of conversation that might
> touch politics or religion and the concealment of every-
> thing that in fact divided them. (Wright, 1987, 152)

If the first quotation captures something of the ideal of face-
to-face interaction, surely the second names what is all too often the
reality. There is a way to move beyond fearful "civility" while both
maintaining the integrity of our own committed identities and
doing respectful justice to the differing, even contradictory, views
and values of others. The metaphor of "conversation" from contemporary hermeneutics offers a guiding image of this way.

In our lives together there are no uninterpreted facts.
Dialogue between people is but one instance of the back-and-forth
movement of questions and answers, agreements and disagreements, confusions and clarifications that characterize all interpretation. The fact that we are typically unaware of this process of
reciprocal interpretation, that so much of interpersonal and inter-
group communication goes on seemingly automatically, makes it
important that we come to an awareness of the ubiquitous process
of "reading" and "being read" in everyday interaction. To be in dialogue is to interpret and be interpreted.

As we first listen to each other's positions, we will find ourselves
agreeing, disagreeing, surprised, or confused in varying combinations
and degrees of intensity. Initial interpretive reactions are an aspect
of all face-to-face communication. They occur as your presentation
of yourself interacts with my expectations, and mine with yours.
These mutual expectations—what each of us takes for granted and

values at the outset of our exchange—partially but importantly account for our initial responses to each other. First impressions are first interpretations. In order to transcend initial impressions, we must have the discipline to temporarily suspend concern with our own position in order to grasp the other's point. Attention to two levels of communication may help us to do so.

Communications research has shown that all face-to-face messages are comprised of content and emotional dimensions. We will better understand each other's positions if we deliberately attend to what each of us is saying and to the signs of its emotional significance. The former is typically conveyed in words, the latter non-verbally in tone of voice, facial expression, posture, and so on. It may also be the case that, in order to grasp each other's points here and now, we may have to work at comprehending the history which has brought us to them. Once again, this requires that we temporarily suspend concern with the delivery of our own views.

The intentional, disciplined, temporary suspension of concern with one's own position is emphatically not to be equated with agreement with the other. In authentic dialogue the extent to which we finally agree and/or disagree must be allowed to emerge from our exchange. The more crucial the matters at stake, the less likely that things will be settled in initial efforts at mutual understanding. The purpose of these efforts at initial understanding is to build a bridge of trust and mutual respect for the subsequent negotiation of legitimate differences in interest and perspective.

When we have done the best we can to understand one another's positions, both initially and in whatever additional depth seems necessary and appropriate, the back-and-forth movement of authentic conversation may now more fruitfully unfold. This will include necessary moments of confrontation and argument, in which real differences are tested. Authentic conversation is a mutual search for truth and fairness. To enter its lists, we must be prepared to subject all positions to a critical and creative suspicion, by means of which the systematic biases on both sides may be exposed and challenged. Those seeking mutual conversation must be prepared, in the words of David Tracy cited above, "to change our minds if the evidence suggests it."

Genuine communication is characterized as much by a willingness to modify one's own position in the light of convincing communication from another, as by the commitment to present one's own position and its warrants unapologetically. The capacity to be affected is as truly a sign of integrity as the capacity to have effects. Because of its thoroughly mutual character, participants in authentic interaction cannot know in advance what its outcomes will be. If we know how a prospective dialogue must (or must not) turn out, we have foreclosed the possibility of becoming caught up in the give-and-take of authentic conversation. What we can know in advance of any human interaction is that genuine receptivity to the other, including the painful possibility that the other's perspective may expose inadequacies in our own, is the necessary requirement for mutual conversion of heart and therefore for the reconciliation of differences.

As we jointly pursue the issue with which we are engaged in the back-and-forth movement named conversation, we are continually confirming, negating, confusing, or bringing each other up short. We are constantly making each other aware of similarities and differences between our respective positions. To allow what we habitually take for granted to be provoked and to risk provoking the other, and to sustain ongoing relationship when such mutual provocation occurs are the fundamental requirements of an authentic life with others. To behave otherwise is to seal ourselves off from the ongoing stream of revelation of which receptive and assertive mutual encounter is the wellspring. If we would say with Buber that in the realm of interpersonal relations, as elsewhere, "all real living is meeting," we must add in the same breath that all meeting is mutual interpretation. There is no such thing as uninterpreted meeting in which we stand before each other as naked facts.

As we insisted in chapter 1, conversation requires a receptivity to otherness which always puts our world of meaning at risk. The source of that risk is clear: The other's communication has the power to affect our worldview, that overarching interpretation of life itself by means of which we maintain coherent meaning.

> We say that we "conduct" a conversation, but the more genuine a conversation is, the less its conduct lies within the will of either partner. Thus a genuine conversation is never the one that we wanted to conduct. Rather, it is generally more correct to say that we fall into conversation, or

even that we become involved in it. The way one word
follows another, with the conversation taking its own
twists and reaching its own conclusion, may well be conducted in some way, but the partners conversing are far
less the leaders of it than the led. (Gadamer, 1990, 383)

To have the meaning of one's very existence called into question is
the ultimate risk for creatures of meaning. There may be no one
with greater power to confirm or disconfirm our identities and values than those in the category of "enemy."

No less is it the case that mutual interaction requires that we
be prepared to indicate plainly where we stand on an issue and why.
Mere receptivity is no basis for creative mutual conversation. The
risk associated with disclosing, and where necessary defending, our
views and values must be borne. Complete other-centeredness is
not only illusory, but signals the abdication of one of the two pri-
mordial responsibilities of our relational lives. It is a failure of mutuality. The receptive and assertive solidarity that can grow out of
sustained mutual relations requires exchanges in mutual vulnerability. Such exchanges lie beyond collusive "civility" and inevitably put
it at risk. It is perhaps not a coincidence that a poet born in the profoundly divided city of Belfast "between the mountain and the
gantries" expressed so beautifully the subjective experience and ultimate significance of having one's world put under question
(Macneice, 1979, 195).

> Yet each of us has known mutations in the mind
> When the world jumped and what had been a plan
> Dissolved and rivers gushed from what had seemed a
>   pool.
> For every static world that you or I impose
> Upon the real one must crack at times and new
> Patterns from new disorders open like a rose
> And old assumptions yield to new sensation;
> The Stranger in the wings is waiting for his cue,
> The fuse is always laid to some annunciation.

Receptivity to otherness even at the cost of extreme provocation to
the world we take for granted, coupled with the willingness to risk

the vulnerability associated with appropriate disclosure of one's own view: such is the double-edged ascetical discipline of authentic dialogue between persons and communities. As we meet in the reciprocally interpretive encounters of everyday life, the stranger in the wings is indeed waiting for a cue; the fuse is always laid to some annunciation. The ground of all such meeting is conversation.

While our focus here is on the particular form of conversation that goes on in an authentic SCC, we want to observe that the quality of conversation that constitutes the life of the larger institutional church requires the same attention to conversational dynamics. A church that for obvious reasons has been guided by a Eurocentric self-interpretation is now opening itself to becoming a world church. It will take new modes of conversation to allow the genius of the Gospel to become incarnate in cultures in ways we never could have imagined. In order for Christianity to move out of Jewish confines, God worked through Peter's dreams to assure us that God plays no cultural favorites. That means putting cultural presuppositions at risk, and with them, cultural appropriations of Christian discipleship. The Spirit is asking a lot these days.

The practical fruit of mutual meetings is the difference they make for the subsequent directions of our lives. Possible futures, ways that our lives might unfold, inevitably surface in authentic dialogue, in the form of invitation and confrontation. Those possibilities then await our response.

The genuinely mutual exchange that we have here named conversation, which is difficult under any circumstances, becomes integrity-threatening under conditions of communal strife. The negotiation of fundamental interests of respect and inclusion is muted because a more primal interest—the community's survival—is put at risk in honestly dealing with such basic human interests. The "civility" which persons pragmatically and understandably adopt so as not to have everyday peace and security continually threatened by escalating cycles of animosity is finally a collusion in denial. Such collusion results when the world is not safe for the sacred game of conversation with its admittedly hard rules and necessary vulnerabilities. Collusion and denial in the name of civility will never move persons with differing interests toward solutions responsive to the legitimate interests of all. Only the honest revelation and disciplined receptivity of real conversation can do that.

Receptivity to otherness in interpersonal conversation requires a willingness to have our interpretation of life put at risk. Others may be carrying a message which will force us into the painful realization that something else might, and perhaps should, be the case with our life. They may come bearing a radical affirmation of our existence. It may be that both things happen. Only the meeting will tell. Our name for such meeting, which we take to be integral to the vitality of any small community of faith, is conversation.

Levels of Mutuality in Conversation

In recent New Testament theology the expression "discipleship of equals" has gained currency, in large measure from the work of Elisabeth Schüssler Fiorenza. We mentioned earlier that God reminded Peter in a dream that God never plays favorites. Paul's expression of the discipleship of equals is unequivocal: for those baptized in Christ Jesus, privilege can neither be granted nor withheld because of ethnicity, social standing, or gender— "There is no longer Jew or Greek, there is no longer slave or free, there is no longer male and female; for all of you are one in Christ Jesus" (Gal 3:28). The level ground of discipleship is the ultimate rationale for mutuality. The language of mutuality is the language of grace.

The basic relational option facing members of intentional community is to enter into conversation with one another or not. Conversation does not occur when we are unable to let others know about our point of view appropriately or when we let our frame of reference and agenda be the only, or at least the most important, one involved in communication with others. Conversation is made possible but is also limited by the capacity of persons to share their perceptions, feelings, wants, needs, beliefs, and knowledge appropriately with each other, and to understand accurately and to respect the differences that exist among them as these emerge. In mutual conversation within SCCs, persons engage in direct and non-manipulative interaction, with each attempting to understand and respect the frame of reference of others. Controlling and being-controlled are rejected as ways of being in relationship, and consensus among respectful equals—being of one mind—is the preferred mode of making communal decisions. Disagreement and conflict call for genuine negotiation.

In order for mutual conversation to characterize relationships among a community's members, those involved must be able and willing to tell their own stories, including the accompanying feelings; to understand accurately the events and feelings of other members' stories; to give constructive positive and negative feedback at appropriate moments; and to receive feedback with a measure of openness. Disclosure, empathy, giving feedback, and receiving feedback are thus the four basic moments of mutual conversation. Together they constitute the necessary everyday way of communicating together in SCCs. Please note the word "necessary" in the previous sentence. Without an adequate level of mutuality in its ongoing conversation, a group should not call itself a community. Note also that the other three core conversations of SCCs discussed in the previous chapter—with the social world as it is, with other groups and institutions in the web of mediating structures, and with the Christian tradition—are likewise necessary conditions. Considered alone, each of these four aspects is a necessary but insufficient condition for authentic Christian community; taken together, these four interrelated conversations constitute such a community.

The four moments of mutual conversation described above involve two basic levels. Disclosure and accurate empathetic understanding constitute a primary level of conversation. At this level, most of the time I will appropriately and directly tell you where I am as regards the issue at hand; you will understand my disclosure from my point of view and indicate your understanding to me. Most of the time you will say where you are and I will receive your statement accurately. These reciprocal behaviors feed on each other: If you want to encourage me to tell you where I stand, one effective way is to give me access to *your* position and experience. If I want you to understand me from *my* perspective, I can try to walk in your shoes for a time. Engaging in these reciprocal behaviors consistently establishes a level of decency, trust, and care in human relationships. This is the basic or foundational level of mutual conversation.

Giving and receiving feedback move conversation to a deeper level of mutuality, one in which, for the most part, I will convey my interpretation of a situation, of your behavior, or of events in our relationship appropriately and directly; and you will consider what I am saying with genuine openness prior to deciding whether you agree with my view. Most of the time you will be willing to give me similar feedback and I will receive it as a gift for my consideration. Like self-disclosure and empathy, the giving and receiving of feedback also reinforce each other. If you want me to give you clear, direct, and specific feedback, it will help if you can offer such feedback to me. If I want you to take my feedback on board openly, I will try to do the same with your feedback to me. Engaging in these reciprocal behaviors consistently and well makes our relationship one of significant belonging and mutually creative transformation.

We describe the first level of mutual conversation as basic because engaging in it is what makes it possible to move to the deeper level. If we want our community's inner life to grow to the deeper conversational level, we must consistently cultivate the primary one. For example, if you want me to take your feedback with openness, be sure that I have first experienced your understanding. At the primary level of conversation we demonstrate basic respect and care for each other; at the secondary level we invite each other to ongoing creative transformation. Engaging consistently in primary level mutuality earns us the right to move to deeper levels of conversation.

The notion of four moments points out the building blocks of genuine conversation; the concept of two levels helps us to see conversation as a dynamic process at work between and among persons. Both aspects are crucial to a vital inner life in an SCC, and both are the product of an ongoing commitment.

If the members of an intentional Christian community are to move toward mutual conversation as the standard in their life together, five interrelated factors must come into play: self-esteem, working knowledge, skills, values, and norms. The absence of any of these factors is sufficient to account for a lack of mutuality within the community's web of relationships; the presence to some degree of all of them is the vital bedrock of vital and creative conversation in SCCs.

Every human group is composed of persons with particular strengths and weaknesses as conversation partners. As we participate in various groups in our everyday lives, our communication skills may develop or diminish, but whatever happens in that regard is ordinarily haphazard. By contrast, the shared life of an SCC offers an ongoing experiential location wherein the capacity for conversation of every member, and therefore the overall depth and quality of mutual interaction within the entire community, can be deliberately and systematically enhanced. In the area of communication, among others, small communities that are working are also learning communities that are working.

Trust in relationships between and among members of an intentional Christian community is both a cause and an effect of mutuality. A kind of basic trust is required before we will risk disclosing ourselves to others, yet disclosing ourselves to others is one important factor in building trust among us. If the basis for trust inside us as individuals and among us as community members is quite limited, our capacity to let ourselves be known in community will be similarly limited. There is no more adequate way to build trust among us than to foster mutuality among us.

We close this discussion with a final word on conversation, intimacy, and mutuality. A perusal of the "self-help" section of any bookstore would reveal that the language and imagery just used—"disclosure," "empathy," "vulnerability," and so on—is also invoked by the many authors writing today on the subject of intimacy. We, however, are not using "conversation" as a synonym for "intimacy" and believe that it is not helpful to do so. So what's the difference? We believe that the term intimacy is best reserved for the level of mutual exposure and vulnerability that we ordinarily associate only with the deepest relationships which can occur between two people. Intimacy, as we understand the term, is best reserved as a name for what happens between spouses, family members, and friends; it is a level of self-revelation and response which would simply be inappropriate not only in the workplace, but also in SCC gatherings. We understand intimacy as two-person conversation at the deepest level; it is not and cannot be a group event. Such a depth of exposure and vulnerability is not a requirement for vital communication within an SCC and to assume that is to misunderstand what constitutes appropriate self-revelation in small community life. To speak quite plainly, someone who joins an SCC primarily in search of intimacy as we have just defined it is looking in the wrong place. We can summarize our view on this point in the following way: authentic intimacy always entails conversation, but authentic conversation need not be intimate. The mutuality necessary for any good conversation, not intimacy, is the appropriate standard for interaction in SCCs.

Consensus

As we noted in introducing this chapter, there is no prefabricated plan for creating a community's inner and public life; these are matters about which community members must come to agreement. Within a community of mature adults, there is no one else to make those decisions. It is within the dynamic ebb and flow of conversation as defined above that community members seek mutually acceptable decisions regarding the shape of their inner and public commitments and the proper balance between them. The quality of our conversation sets the limit for the quality of our arriving at consensus. And because these matters cannot be settled simply once and for all in a dynamic community that exists within an ever-changing world, the work of arriving at and revising consensus is ongoing.

By "consensus" we mean the process of arriving at shared decisions that are maximally respectful and inclusive of the different points of view, priorities, and values of members. Consensus, then, is a form of *joint* decision-making. As such it may be contrasted with two other forms. In *autonomous* decision-making, the designated leader of a group decides things by him- or herself. In *consultative* decision-making, the designated leader makes decisions, but only after conferring with other group members. In the form of joint decision-making, which we here call consensus, no one person or subgroup of people decides things for the community. Decisions are shared.

Group Conditions for Consensus

Paul often asks members of the various Christian communities that they commit themselves to being of one mind and that the one mind should be that of Jesus Christ. It would be a very naive reading to suppose he meant that there must always be total agreement on all points. We know from the words Paul uses—variations of the Greek verb *phronein*—that a better rendering might be this: the meaning of the world and our life together in the world should be a basic point of agreement, and Jesus Christ is the touchstone of meaning. That is the ultimate call to consensus.

But Christians must engage in particular strategies that help build a particular world out of meanings they co-own. That particular world might be about what a family does, how two friends structure their friendship, what decisions a parish council makes for the life of the parish, how a union is organized, and so on. So, functionally, we also have to reach consensus on many issues other than just the basic meanings out of which we live.

Researchers and experienced practitioners have identified a number of group conditions that foster high-quality consensus decision-making: unity of purpose; equal access to power; autonomy from external, hierarchical structures; time; willingness to attend to process and attitudes; and willingness to learn and practice the skills required for consensus decision-making (Avery, Auvine, Streibel, and Weiss, 1981, 19–21). Each of these bear brief elaboration given the context and purposes of this book.

Without unity of purpose, the attempt to seek group consensus is like having two people on either side of a boat row alternately—the boat ends up going in circles. In the context of an SCC we suggest that "unity of purpose" means a level of shared affirmation of the basic commitments to *koinonia*, *diakonia*, *leitourgia*, and *kerygma* as discussed in chapter 3. The specific ways in which those commitments are to be met are exactly that about which the community must seek consensus. Like so many other dimensions of SCC life (for example, the relationship between trust and mutual conversation mentioned above), unity of purpose and shared decision-making both require and strengthen each other. As our capacity to arrive at inclusive, respectful, creative consensus deepens, so does our unity of purpose; as our unity of purpose grows, so does our ability to seek and find agreement.

Equal access to power is and ought to be one of the hallmarks of SCCs; they are perhaps today's most powerful context for realizing a discipleship of equals. Indeed, the wish for shared power as adult members of a community of faith is one of the great attractions which SCCs hold for their members. This undoubtedly has much to do with an acutely felt exclusion from power in most persons' experience of both church and society. Equal access to decisional power is particularly significant in addressing the pervasive sexism that women have routinely experienced in church membership, as well as the clericalism which has long denied lay people full participation in the body of Christ. In faithfully and resolutely engaging in the practice of shared decision-making, adult members of SCCs can reclaim a power of baptism that was always rightfully theirs and learn to exercise it gracefully.

The issue of freedom from external, hierarchical structures flows directly from the previous point. As we noted in chapter 3, while all SCCs in the U.S. are outside the traditional mode of parish life, they have made their appearance in both more mainstream and more marginal forms. Its relationship to the church's institutional structure characterizes an SCC as one or the other. Mainstream SCCs are formed within and ordinarily maintain strong connections to the matrix of parish or congregational life. Marginal communities take their stand outside parish or congregation, in a way that implies dissatisfaction with and critique of typical patterns of governance, worship, service, or fellowship. Both forms of SCC have emerged as a response to what is and is not occurring in institutional church practice and stand to some degree outside of the hierarchical structure. For that reason they will often and understandably experience varying states of tension with it. Tension is one source of growth in all healthy relationships.

Arriving at decisions via consensus ordinarily takes more time than autonomous or consultative decision-making. It takes time for a group to clarify its understanding of an issue to be decided, as well as to share differing interpretations of the problem, its place within an overall set of priorities, and possible solutions. In any reasonably lively community, differences will be present in all these areas and more. A consensus decision requires weaving those differences together into a unique whole that could not have been arrived at by any individual group member precisely because it emerged from the members' conversation. Such a process can and does yield unpredictable and creative results, but only when a community is willing to put in the time to engage in it deeply, patiently, wisely, and respectfully.

A willingness to attend to process and attitudes supportive of consensus means that members of an SCC must be as concerned with the quality of their engagement with each other in consensus-building as they are with its particular outcomes; also, they must note and respond appropriately to indicators of whether or not members are fully engaged with community decision-making. Research in small group dynamics suggests that satisfying process and constructive attitudes are signs that the group is dealing adequately with four recurring issues of such dynamics: inclusion, power, closeness, and collaboration. We will examine these issues later in this chapter.

Finally, a willingness to learn and practice relevant skills is a crucial condition for building the capacity for reaching good agreements within an SCC. A "skill" is simply a behavior that we are able to engage in at will when it is appropriate. First and foremost the skills required for consensus are those of good conversation partners as discussed above: self-disclosure, empathy, constructive feedback, and receptivity to others' views. Beyond these there are other particular skills that seeking consensus requires, such as brainstorming and collaborative planning. In SCCs the gift of these various skills will have been distributed throughout the membership by the Spirit in different measures. Given a consistent climate of mutual conversation and an ongoing commitment to decisions based on consensus, these gifts strengthen and multiply.

Steps in Building Consensus

There is, of course, no formula guaranteed to produce a good agreement among people. There are as many models for consensus available as there are for communication, leadership, intimacy, and so on. The following series of steps, drawn from the literature on consensus and our own experience in SCCs and other small groups, offers one way of conceiving how an SCC might seek consensus on any issue it faces. The "subject" of each of the following sentences is the community; a word will follow on the role of facilitators.

1. Specify clearly the decision to be made.
2. Provide all members with relevant background information at the outset of discussion and as necessary along the way.
3. Seek necessary clarifications regarding the decision and background information before proceeding to deliberate.

4. Converse together about what the community should decide given the available background information.
5. Encourage all members to express their provisional views of the matter, including both possible solutions and value priorities.
6. Use a brainstorming process to generate a list of possible choices.
7. Identify the preferred choice(s) of the group at this juncture.
8. If there is more than one preferred choice at this juncture, explore each further, then test again for consensus.
9. Should consensus not be reached at this point, the community can decide to adopt a choice now because to do otherwise would have negative consequences, or to postpone a decision to allow for further prayer, reflection, and conversation on the matter.

Whoever is facilitating the community's conversation while consensus is being sought is responsible for keeping the conversation on the subject, clarifying statements by community members, encouraging participation, summarizing developing positions, and moving the conversation through the steps just outlined in a timely but flexible manner. She or he or they must either take themselves out of the decision-making process except as facilitator (that is, keep their opinions on the decision at hand to themselves), or refrain from allowing their own views of the matter at hand to influence their role in the process unduly. The reason that many experienced facilitators choose the former option is that the latter is often quite difficult and sometimes impossible.

We have stressed that a willingness to attend to process and attitudes is a necessary condition for strong shared decision-making. Following is a paraphrase of "Rules for Building United Judgment" from the Institute for Nonviolence Education, Research, and Training (cited in Avery et al., 1981, 14). It is eloquently expressive of the spirit which must ground the behaviors just outlined if creative consensus-building is to become a seasoned and integral dimension of the life of small Christian communities.

1. The spirit of consensus is that of a calm, hospitable gathering of friends to determine truth, rather than a tense contest to see which side can prevail.
2. When the meeting becomes tense or when people begin to repeat themselves, wait in silence.
3. If nothing new emerges or if the atmosphere is becoming unfriendly and pressured, suspend judgment and agree to return to the matter again.
4. Take no action as a group until the matter has been satisfactorily resolved for all members of the group.
5. Be willing to repeat this process patiently as often and as long as it takes to find a mutually acceptable solution.

The above advice notwithstanding, we are not advocates of a rigid or "pure" model of reaching consensus. That is, we do not believe that an SCC should always refrain from decisions until all members wholeheartedly agree. While that might be desirable, total agreement is rare in the real world and not necessary for vital group life. A "good enough" agreement is the standard we propose for SCCs seeking consensus. We simply mean that, while all members of the community may not fully agree with a particular course of action, they feel that their views have been respectfully considered and can live with the choice in good faith. A member not in full agreement with a particular choice may nevertheless opt to go along with it because he or she realizes that to do so is preferable to doing nothing. It is, of course, possible that situations may arise where a member may choose to leave the community rather than assent to a particular agreement. We have seen such choices made in an atmosphere of respect for the integrity of all involved. Our conviction that "good enough" consensus is good enough is partly based on the assumption noted above that in the life of a vital SCC the process of coming to agreements is as important as the actual agreements reached.

A final word on this important subject. Remember that consensus is a moment within a more fundamental process named conversation. When community members are seeking consensus—just as when they are sharing their faith, engaging in social analysis, or supporting one another through difficult times—they are in conversation with each other. So the keys to reaching satisfying, creative, respectful agreements are appropriate disclosure, accurate empathy, constructive feedback, and receptivity to feedback. Shared decisions characterized by wisdom, creativity, respect, and integrity arise among conversation partners who learn to speak the truth in love to one another and be receptive to such speaking.

Conflict

Conflict is present in any community. The writings of Paul frequently address divisions in the early Christian community, outlining fundamental attitudes needed to deal with conflict. From Acts we learn that conflict was there in the beginning. Conflict between John Mark and Paul made Paul refuse to engage in missionary travel with him. An entire chapter in Matthew's Gospel is devoted to conflict and reconciliation. Matthew insists that being forgiven by God depends upon our own abilities to reconcile with each other. Community, like all friendship and love, is never free of conflict.

Yet conflict has a bad reputation in polite company generally and in Christian company particularly. Many adult Christians grew up with the sense that angry outbursts were sins. These adults often unknowingly continue to have the limits of their understanding and their ability to deal with conflict set by childhood experiences. Thus their experience of conflict is laden with unresolved feelings of anxiety, sadness, anger, and shame. As a consequence some of us flee conflict as we would the Ebola virus, some of us seek out every opportunity to replay the unresolved battles of childhood in nonproductive ways, while most of us deal with conflict when we have to, but we'd much prefer to have it leave us alone.

A colleague of ours, an expert in negotiation, entitles one of his seminars not "Conflict Resolution" or "Conflict Management" but "Conflict Utilization" because of his judgment that conflict situations are valuable, perishable moments in the life of groups and institutions. We want to explore his countercultural intuition a bit farther as the prelude to this section. Rather than error, breakdown, or sin, conflict is better understood as a state that arises naturally because of differences in people's assumptions, perceptions, needs, feelings, thoughts, values, expectations, goals, and so on. Where there are differences, there will be conflict. A group that is conflict-free has somehow suppressed its awareness of its differences beneath a facade of shared vision. It has also deprived itself of its primary source of growth. Recall for a moment our discussion above of the crucial place of the "other" in the life of conversation. We find out far more about who we are, about our strengths as well as our limitations, in the presence of one who differs from us than we do in interacting with someone who shares much of what we already know and believe. The truth of this observation is best illustrated by the phenomenon of cults, in which uniqueness and therefore diversity must be surrendered at the gate as a condition of belonging. Once that surrender is made, there is no "other" to let us see ourselves. There is only more of the same.

Even if we were able to reevaluate conflict so that it began to appear to us as a resource to be utilized for growth, we would still face the question of how to respond constructively. Our purpose in this section is to share one well-tested and highly regarded model for dealing well with the opportunities which conflicts provide. In 1981 Roger Fisher and William Ury of the Harvard Negotiation Project published a book entitled *Getting to Yes: Negotiating Agreement without Giving In*. It has since become the most widely used and frequently cited practical resource in the English-speaking world for dealing with conflict. As fate, or more likely the tastes of popular culture would have it, another best-selling work on negotiation entitled *Looking Out for Number One* was published at the same time. A perceptive review in *Newsweek* magazine nailed the difference between the two books squarely on the head. The underlying philosophy of the latter work is clearly revealed in its provocative title: Negotiation is about getting as much of what you want as you can, and to negotiate is to look out for your own interests. We need not deny the partial truth of this view, even as we recognize its grievous inadequacy. The underlying assumption about negotiation in *Getting to Yes* is, however, quite different. The authors refer to the process taught in their book as "principled negotiation." The principle which underpins their method is that a good agreement must respond fairly to the legitimate interests of both parties and that it is in both parties' interest that any agreement meets the needs of all involved, especially when negotiation goes on in the context of a continuing relationship. It is a principle which we endorse in the context of SCCs, perhaps not least because it is so profoundly congruent with the biblical injunction to love the neighbor as the self. Indeed, it provides community members with a quite straightforward means of moving that injunction from notion to behavior.

The method of principled negotiation of conflict involves four steps, which we shall describe and illustrate. The first step is to **focus on issues, not on personalities.** When we find ourselves in the presence of difference that becomes conflict, it seems quite natural to hone in on the other—their stubbornness, selfishness, shortsightedness, need to control—as if that were where the problem lay. Our challenge then is to overcome or overwhelm these limitations in the other, who meanwhile is of course typically doing the same thing on their side: that is, seeing *our* personal shortcomings as the source of the conflict and responding accordingly. These are not propitious vantage points from which to resolve differences since they quickly, indeed instantaneously, spawn circular arguments. The wife who says to her husband "I'd be much more willing to cut down on my drinking if you weren't nagging me about it all the time" is very likely to receive the following rejoinder: "If you would just cut down a little on the drinking, I wouldn't have to hassle you about it so much." From her perspective the source of the problem is his nagging, from his it is her drinking. As long as they hold to their respective views and act accordingly, the outcome—an escalating vicious cycle of mutual misunderstanding, blame, and defensiveness—is highly predictable. Chronic conflicts between persons and groups very often involve this process of an escalating, circular focus on the "other-as-problem."

The simple, but not easy, alternative to the trap of mutual blame is to shift the focus of conversation from personalities to the issues on which the parties differ. Fisher and Ury offer four communicative guidelines for accomplishing this:

1. *"Listen actively and acknowledge what is being said."* Nothing interrupts the unproductive process of focusing on and blaming the other more expeditiously than working to understand and convey to them our comprehension of their position. One person cannot actively listen to and acknowledge another and blame them at the same time. When either party caught up in a cycle of mutual blame stops, the entire process is interrupted. And as we insisted in our

treatment of conversation above, to understand another's view is neither to agree with it nor to surrender one's own.

2. *"Speak to be understood."* The emotional pressures and intensities of conflict too often lead us to speak aggressively or defensively, rather than to explain our position as simply and clearly as possible. Like listening actively, speaking to be understood often interrupts an unproductive focus on the other's shortcomings. To be understood is not to dominate or to win, but to represent one's position assertively and fairly.

3. *"Speak about yourself, not about them."* It is unfortunate that this insight has been trivialized in the self-help and personal-growth literature into an unnuanced exhortation to make "I statements." In the context of negotiation, the importance of speaking about your own experience is captured in the difference between accusing someone of selfishness and naming your disappointment, hurt, or anger in response to a specific action of theirs. The latter is harder to dismiss.

4. *"Speak for a purpose."* The anxiety provoked by conflict often pushes people toward two extremes, either "running off at the mouth" or withdrawing into muteness. In an emotion-laden situation too much disclosure makes it difficult to negotiate, and too little makes it impossible. To negotiate well, we need a reasonably clear awareness of what we are trying to accomplish and the skill and assertiveness to name our goal at the right time, neither under- nor overstating our position.

These four behaviors give us valuable guidance on how to focus on issues rather than personalities. The best way to invite the other into this way of negotiating is simple: Do it yourself. To do so is to take the first step in principled negotiation.

The second step in principled negotiation is to **focus on interests, not positions.** In teaching small community members and leaders to recognize and utilize this difference over the past ten years, we have come to the judgment that this is the most insightful point in this remarkably valuable model of constructive negotiation. People who understand the difference between interests and positions and who can put their understanding into action are well on their way to utilizing conflict creatively. Fisher and Ury teach this point most effectively by way of the following story:

… two men [are] quarreling in a library. One wants the window open and the other wants it closed. They bicker back and forth about how much to leave it open; a crack, halfway, three quarters of the way. No solution satisfies them both.

Enter the librarian. She asks one why he wants the window open; "To get some fresh air." She asks the other why he wants the window closed: "To avoid the draft." After thinking a minute, she opens wide a window in the next room, bringing in fresh air without a draft. (Fisher and Ury, 1981, 41)

Those who seek to utilize conflict as a source of growth through a process of principled negotiation will do well to remember and reflect on this parable. "I want the window open" is a position; "to get some fresh air" is an interest. "I want the window closed" is a position; "to avoid the draft" is an interest. A *position*, then, may be defined as a proposed resolution to a problem or choice facing two or more people, while an *interest* may be defined as the agenda underlying a position. One key to dealing with conflict creatively is not letting your positions override your interests!

The authors of *Getting to Yes* make a persuasive argument that all too often what passes for negotiation is actually a process of compromising mechanically between positions. If I have a car to sell and am asking $2000 for it, and you offer me $1600, it would not be unusual for us to strike a bargain by "splitting the difference," that is, compromising between our respective starting points by agreeing to a sale price of $1800. It just seems fair to proceed in this fashion, doesn't it? But what if my initial position or yours was really a bargaining ploy, having nothing to do with the market value of the car? As long as we simply shift positions in the effort to compromise, the merits of what is being negotiated need never arise. Perhaps such "positional bargaining" works reasonably well in one-time transactions like selling a used car to a stranger, but how do we split the difference between positions when we are in conflict about the division of labor and rewards in our workplace, or an acceptable balance between career and family commitments in a marriage, or the tension between inner and public commitments in an SCC?

Simple positional compromise is typically not much help in such circumstances because it does not allow us to get to the interests underlying real-life conflicts. Fisher and Ury propose that a reliable way to move from positions to interests is to look at any position and ask why it is being taken. Toward what ends are negotiators taking their respective positions? What are they trying to accomplish, that is, what are their interests? We have observed, for example, that in many contemporary SCCs an almost predictable tension can arise between women and men around a variety of inner and public issues. From the perspective of principled negotiation, this suggests that beneath the surface of conflicting positions on specific matters lie more basic conflicting interests. The interest underlying this tension often proves to involve the recognition of the equal talents and rights of women to exercise leadership in all aspects of the life of the community. No amount of compromising on positions will make this fundamental issue go away. It must be addressed forthrightly as a fundamental question pervading all community decisions. Two-thousand years of patriarchal disrespect and disempowerment cannot be exorcised by polite compromise. A much more demanding conversation is required of those who would see that pattern brought to a halt. And one of the places where it is being halted today is among women and men in small communities of faith.

Because a good agreement is one which is responsive to the legitimate interests of all parties involved, engaging in principled negotiation entails being clear about our respective interests. (The word "legitimate" in this context simply indicates our recognition that dominating or disrespecting another is never a legitimate negotiating interest.) Community members must become adept both at recognizing why they are advocating a particular decision during a consensus-building process and at recognizing other members' interests as well. In doing so they should recall that parties in conflict always have not one but rather a range of interests. Some of these will be shared between them, some will be unrelated, and some will be in conflict. Good consensus decision-making explores this range of interests, seeking possible agreements responsive to legitimate concerns of all parties.

A last word on the subject of interests. Fisher and Ury remind us that we usually have two kinds of interests as negotiators, resolving the issue at hand and sustaining our relationship with the other for the future. In SCCs, where *koinonia* is a fundamental commitment, the interest in sustaining relationships is strongly present in all attempts to negotiate. The method of principled negotiation teaches that the best way to strengthen a relationship for the future is to negotiate mutually respectful agreements in the present.

The third step in principled negotiation is to **invent options for mutual gain**. "Mutual gain" means "responsive to the interests of all parties." If the relevant interests have been well articulated and understood by both sides, the next step is to craft possible agreements that are responsive to those interests. This ordinarily requires generating a list of possibilities, prioritizing them in relationship to the relevant interests, and compromising as necessary so that all parties' interests are recognized in the final agreement. Compromise around interests is the "real stuff" of all negotiations: How do we fairly and wisely balance the differing, legitimate interests of all parties by creating an agreement with which we all can live? As we hope the foregoing explanation makes clear, attempting to compromise by merely adjusting positions actually keeps parties with differences from getting to an exploration of their real interests, and, therefore, precludes the possibility of seeking new options for mutual benefit.

The authors of *Getting to Yes* suggest that negotiators who invent options for mutual gain have figuratively shifted from facing each other over the problem across the table to sitting side by side with the problem in front of them to be jointly resolved. As in the wonderful story of the library windows, there are often other possible positions than the ones which the parties initially take. Once again the caution is clear: Do not let your positions defeat your interests.

The fourth and final step in the process of principled negotiation is to **agree on criteria for monitoring the agreement.** This simply means specifying who is responsible for doing what and by what time. Experienced negotiators and mediators are well aware that what is accomplished in the arduous work of the first three negotiating steps can be lost if the parties involved fail to agree concretely and unambiguously about what each will do and the timeline for doing it. Agreements don't work just because they have been reached; they work when they are implemented. The underlying interest here is accountability. Specifying criteria for monitoring an agreement allows the parties involved to practice mutual accountability. These criteria reduce the possibility that at a later date one or the other party can say "I didn't realize that that's what you expected me to do," or "We never agreed to a specific date." There is no genuine consent without agreement, and no effective agreement without specific commitments.

We ask you to remember that conflict, like consensus, is a moment within the ongoing process of conversation within a web of relationships; it is not a sign that something is wrong, but that there are differences present which must be addressed. An SCC's capacity to deal with conflict sets a limit on the depth and quality of its inner life. For any community (indeed, any relationship) the question is not whether there is such a limit, but rather where it is. Like families and friendships, SCCs unravel when problems are not addressed forthrightly. Members of a community that has never experienced a significant conflict have simply not drawn close enough to each other to warrant being called a community. Engaging in the disciplined form of conversation called principled negotiation allows community members to test the limit which their differences are placing on their relationships.

A final, pointed suggestion: Get a copy of *Getting to Yes*, read it together, and put it in your SCC's library!

Leadership

Communication goes on from the first instant of the first meeting of an SCC until the last moment of its final meeting. We have tried to show here that the foundational task in creating a vibrant inner life in a community is to make communication become conversation. Seeking consensus and utilizing conflict are critical examples of communication becoming conversation. The third is leadership.

The Lilly research project on SCCs revealed that the communities studied reported little in the way of explicitly established patterns over time to guide the exercise of initiative and influence within them. Within the most common, parish-connected type of SCC, nearly half chose leaders by asking for volunteers; only 18 percent used some kind of discernment to choose their leaders. This penchant toward casual selection may reflect wariness based on troubling experiences within hierarchical structures of designated leadership. Leadership is too important to be neglected or treated casually, and so we turn our explicit focus on it here.

Our common understanding of leadership has gone though stages (Whitehead and Whitehead, 1986). Leadership was once regarded as a personality trait given to certain people, but not others ("followers"). Later it was conceived of as involving the relationship between leaders and individual followers. Leaders led individuals by giving them tasks that stretched them developmentally. More recently leadership has been understood as a group phenomenon. Leaders see to it that the functional needs of the group regarding its relationships and tasks are addressed. The emerging understanding of leadership views leadership as a process of interaction, which might be called "leading/following" within a group. In the words of the Whiteheads, leadership "includes everything that goes on in the group that contributes to its effectiveness" (p. 75). This analysis suggests that leadership in SCCs should not be thought of as anyone's individual prerogative based on personality or designated role, but rather as a process of interaction among all community members to which each can contribute according to his or her talents and inclinations.

The literature on small groups and our own experience with small communities suggest that there is a certain predictability to what SCC members will find themselves conversing about. This predictable sequence has enormous implications for leadership as SCCs develop. In a splendid essay entitled "Leadership and Power," our colleague Evelyn Eaton Whitehead draws on contemporary psychological studies of small group development to identify four recurring issues in the life of all groups: inclusion, power, closeness, and effectiveness. While all four issues are always present in the life of a group, they tend to come into focus at different times, in a somewhat predictable sequence. "The best image perhaps," she writes, "is one of shifting priorities: at different moments in our life together as a group, different questions come to 'center stage' and demand more of our time" (1987, 52). The life of SCCs will predictably involve cycling and recycling through times of primary concern with these issues. Let's look briefly at each of the four basic tasks of group life.

Inclusion is the task of group life that involves members coming to be a part of a group's interaction and feeling as if they belong.

In the absence of most members having a sense of being included, a group will not be able to muster the collective energy necessary to fulfill either side of its mission. In the formative stage of an SCC, hospitality or the personal welcoming of members to the newly forming group is crucial. There is no more profound way of welcoming and including someone in the life of an intentional community than by inviting them to tell their own stories and then acknowledging the contributions that are forthcoming. It is important that anyone functioning as a leader at this juncture share their own stories and hopes for the community's life, for in doing so they identify themselves as conversation partners in an incipient community of equals.

An important way to foster the telling of stories and sharing of gifts is by providing a simple structure to help a community "get going." The literature on small group dynamics demonstrates clearly that such a structure can support and integrate a group while its own inner cohesion has the opportunity to develop. These beginning structures of inclusion must, of course, be in the service of the group and build up its own identity and agenda, rather than promoting anyone's personal agenda. Potential community members will be quite sensitive to which of these approaches is actually operating.

While belonging is inevitably a focal issue in the beginning of an intentional Christian community, inclusion issues will arise from time to time throughout the life of any group. In that sense, as Whitehead's comment quoted above indicates, these issues never go away.

Power is the task of group life in which members learn to engage in mutual influence in a creative, reciprocal fashion. The issue here is how a group enables its members to exercise their different gifts appropriately and potently in the service of the group's mission. Groups always function as more or less than the sum of their individual members. A group's power or influence will similarly be more or less than the individual powers of its members, depending on the kind of leadership resources it mobilizes.

When an intentional Christian community is relatively comfortable as regards inclusion, it becomes highly likely that a contest of influence will emerge. When it does, whoever had been exercising a leadership role may experience a challenge. These contests and challenges vary in their quality and intensity from bitter and hostile attacks to assertive yet respectful proposals of alternative courses of action for the community's life. Evelyn Whitehead reminds us that, far from simply being negative events, this development signals growth in group maturity. She also notes that leaders need not be passive victims of attacks during these inevitable attempts to balance power among us. She writes:

> The designated leader is usually in a position of some considerable power when the first questioning of leadership occurs. If the leader uses that power against the group member who questions, the rest of the group learns that new patterns of power will not be easily won. The message is given that the stakes are high in the process of change. If, however, the designated leader does not respond to this question as if it were a personal attack, a different tale is told. The message here is that power in the group need not be interpreted as a personal possession and jealously guarded from attack. Rather it is a resource of the group that needs to—and can—be examined, accounted for, and even redistributed among us. (1987, 59)

A creative inner life in small Christian communities means embracing and fostering the mutual, reciprocal practice of influence and initiative—the practice of relational power—among community members.

Closeness is the task of group life which involves negotiating an adequate and appropriate degree of personal revelation among members. Because an SCC has some characteristics of a family and some of formal organizations, it must find a level of personal sharing which is suitable to its goals and fits with the needs and preferences of its particular members.

Within some small Christian communities, the sharing of feelings and dreams and the willingness to work on relationships between and among members will tend in a deeply personal direction. Membership in such communities may be a primary source of emotional support and challenge, of companionship and closeness, in the lives of their members. Other communities may give rise to cordial, supportive, but less personally involving relationships, with members finding their primary intimacy connections elsewhere. As long as an adequate degree of mutual conversation is present within a community, either of these options, or any point between the two, offers a perfectly legitimate resolution of the issue of closeness. It is also not uncommon for communities to find that their norms and behaviors around closeness go through significant changes over time, changes that must be worked out in ongoing negotiation.

Dealing well with this issue of group life involves recognizing that differences are likely to exist in members' hopes and fears regarding closeness among them and then negotiating these differences directly, respectfully, and with an appropriate measure of flexibility. At a deeper level, growth in this area calls for an awareness of how the unresolved wounds of past relationships can creates barriers to closeness within an SCC. It also calls for a sense of when these barriers can be appropriately worked on within the community and when outside help is required for individual members or the entire community. Because of the intensely personal character of questions of closeness and the strong feelings they tend to generate in all of us, this issue will put the conversational skills and commitments of community members to the test in a unique way. Leadership in this task of group life requires a particular sensitivity to differing emotional needs and personal modes of expression among group members.

Effectiveness is the task of group life which involves movement from mission to goals to action to evaluation. In these moments of a group's life, Whitehead writes, "its chief priorities now are clarity about its task and the effective use of its resources to meet this goal." If the basic tasks of SCCs are to develop an inner and a public life, then the effectiveness of such communities has to do precisely with the quality of their sustained efforts along those lines.

Leadership in the pursuit of effectiveness is a matter of nurturing the community's sense of mission and vision, fostering community consensus about particular goals, coordinating and stewarding the resources of the community in pursuing its chosen agenda, assisting the community realistically to evaluate its effectiveness, and keeping the results of such evaluation in conversation with the community's mission and vision. Such leadership requires many of the kinds of working knowledge and skills which professional managers

in our society use every day; what is different, of course, is the ultimate context within which members of SCCs locate their concern
for effectiveness. Authentic Christian communities are never concerned with effectiveness for its own sake or for the sake of prof-
itability; they are always concerned with their effectiveness in
inserting the dangerous memories and transformative hopes embedded in the Christian story into their history and society.

The presentation of each of these four issues in sequence may
leave readers with the impression that all are of equal weight or
require the same degree of effort from community members. This
is not the case. While particular communities might find otherwise,
those experienced with small group and community dynamics have
found that the hierarchy of relative difficulty of the four issues is as
follows: power, closeness, effectiveness, and inclusion. Power is the
relatively most difficult issue to deal with, and inclusion the relatively least difficult. Closeness and effectiveness fall somewhere in
between. We are speaking here not of the relative *importance* of
these issues, but of the relative *difficulty* of confronting them. These
shifting patterns of priorities and emphases in the life of vital, developing groups require that SCCs intentionally develop the multi-
plicity of their members' gifts for leadership.

Like gifts for community leadership in facilitating mutual conversation—including both seeking consensus and dealing with conflict creatively—gifts for community leadership in dealing with
issues of inclusion, power, closeness, and effectiveness do not automatically belong to those currently designated as leaders, but are
distributed within the community as a whole. Different moments of
need in the ongoing conversation of the community will call forth
these different gifts.

Closing

We are familiar with the situation in which good people are
unable to accomplish certain tasks because they lack appropriate
skills. That happens to all of us. The skills that facilitate consensus
building and conflict utilization are not just "good business"—they
are redemptive of our life together in Christ Jesus. They may be
our good work, but when they operate within our shared life

because of our commitment to build up the body of Christ, they are works of grace.

Seeking consensus, utilizing conflict, and exercising relational leadership are critical moments within the ongoing conversation which constitutes a small Christian community. Commitments to working collaboratively to forge consensus which respects differences, to seeking reconciliation when difference becomes conflict, and to developing inclusive servant leadership are pledges to stay with conversation—and conversion. That is why the evangelists who gave us the gospels placed such stress on being of one mind, dealing with conflict soundly, and not lording it over each other in their respective communities. Conversation is the way that makes it possible to reject the narrow individualism of the dominant U.S. culture and seek the relational selfhood which appears in the biblical tradition's classic images of a world of just and merciful relationships, a world wherein the neighbor is loved as the self and the widow, orphan, and alien are recognized as siblings, a world of shalom. Conversation requires of SCC members an ongoing receptivity to conversion as they participate in forging their communities' inner and public lives.

6

External Mission:
The Public Life of Small Christian Communities

I want to be guided in developing a spirituality that is not
just private and interpersonal, but also political, institutional and public...I won't want my children to be prepared for receiving the Eucharist without knowing that
the Body of Christ is not only a sacred presence to be
received at the altar on Sunday, but is also a social, political and economic reality that must be nurtured and con-
structed in the wider community.
                                 Ronald Krietemeyer, *Church*, Fall 1991, 13

Introduction

The Christ-event is about God's intentions for our world, for
our life together. The mission of community is incomprehensible in
breadth and variety. Evangelization is a sending that tells the
Christian story where it has never been told before. There is the
evangelization of our culture, family life, workplace, friendships,
and—be it said—of the church itself. We are sent "short distances"
as well as long, on small tasks as well as large.   We are sent on works
of charity. We are sent on works of justice. We are sent on spiritual
works of mercy and corporal works of mercy. Our sending is always
tailored to our gifts and energies. We are not sent at age seventy to
do what we may have been sent to do at age twenty.
    Our emphasis in this chapter is a limited one. We will focus
upon justice issues and the ways that systems function or dysfunction. We will also focus upon the potential of small Christian communities to make a real difference in the shalom or well-being of the

city. This is not the only work of God in human history, but it is a critical one.

Choosing this focus reflects two priorities. The first is that in this century we have come to a far better understanding of the impact of systems upon individual lives. That is why the church has become increasingly articulate about social justice in its teaching voice. As a church, we have a long history of commitment to individual works of charity. These individual works are certainly not being abandoned. But if we meet immediate need on the individual level without addressing the systemic causes of immediate need, we risk extending the life of unjust systems by always being there to "pick up the pieces" of the problems they create.

The second priority comes from our conviction that within U.S. culture we are much more likely to focus upon a community's inner life. Our propensity to form support groups is well documented. In our judgment, a critical challenge to small Christian communities is to move beyond being a support group to develop their faith's effective public life. Therefore, we are paying extended attention to this factor.

A further limitation to the scope of this chapter is that we frequently reflect upon faith's public life from the perspective of very specific experience, that of broad-based community organizing. It's not the only way, but it is a specific way that has been replicated in many others parts of the United States. We speak from this experience because it is *our* experience, and it works—not perfectly, perhaps, but well. Our experience is not the only way of working for the shalom of the city. It is one way.

Faith's Public Life

The purpose of this chapter is to develop the theme of the public life of small Christian communities. We want to provide a framework for thinking socially and religiously about the larger public life of our society and then describe an example of such thinking in action. As we proceed, we will retrieve the previously introduced concept of mediating structures and show how such structures hold the key to small communities of faith forging an authentic public life. We end by describing an effort underway by

SCCs to create a strong public presence through the medium of a broad-based community organization.

Two caveats are important at the doorway to this chapter. First, we have learned that the concept of organizing for power has a way of making white Christians nervous. Western culture thinks of power as something that is unilateral and that does great harm to people and the earth when exercised regularly. This exercise of that form of power would give any thoughtful person pause. Our focus in this chapter is on organizing for power that will be exercised relationally for the common good of a larger community. Second, the principles and practices of confronting failures of justice and mercy should be applied not only in public life of the secular world but also in the public life of the church as well. We are convinced that one of the reasons why the institutional church changes so slowly is that its adult members, both religious and laity, have not yet learned how to exercise their proper authority. They have not yet learned how to help shape church life by addressing prejudiced or capricious institutional decisions. Abuses of power and authority within the institutional church can be effectively confronted only by people who have learned to organize themselves.

As we insisted in chapter 4, the public life of SCCs is about "evoking cries that expect answers" and "learning to address them where they will be taken seriously" (Brueggemann, 1978, 22). It is in forging powerful public partnerships with others seeking the common good of the larger community and of society that SCCs develop their prophetic imaginations and join their voices with others in a prophetic chorus.

We begin exploring how SCCs develop their public side by calling to your attention typical associations to the term "public person." For most of us, what probably comes to mind is one of two kinds of people: celebrities from the arenas of entertainment, sports, or business, or politicians. Bruce Springsteen, Michael Jordan, Reverend Jesse Jackson, and former President Clinton are public people. The concept of public personhood in our time is fed from two streams. The first is notoriety or name recognition, the second is involvement in electoral politics. Sometimes these streams come together in the careers of individuals whose fame in some area of life combines with subsequent involvement in electoral politics. Thus the ultimate "public person" would be the celebrity who becomes a politician—Dwight

Eisenhower, for example, or Ronald Reagan. This is the dominant cultural understanding of publicness in Western democracies today. Understood in this way, you or I or anyone else who is not famous or involved in electoral politics is not a public person.

A more ancient and powerful way of understanding public life, however, sees it as essential to the character of our personhood. This way of understanding recognizes that decisions are made daily within our society that lead to outcomes affecting our whole social body. Let us give one concrete example of such decisions in the area of public education:

There is a large, metropolitan county in the center of the United States which is divided into twenty-three public-school districts. In one of those, more than $8,700 was spent per pupil during a recent school year; in another just over $3,100 was spent per pupil. This pattern repeats itself around the country today wherever great economic differences between urban and suburban living conditions are found, unless decisions have been made at the state or federal level to equalize spending per pupil.

In this book we are defining public life as the arena within our society wherein decisions affecting the common good are made about such matters as job creation, employment, education, health care, housing, and pollution. Public life is the place where citizens and people of faith exercise or fail to exercise our responsibilities for seeking the common good. It is the place where decisions are made which mean:

- that nearly 25 percent of Americans sixteen years old and older are functionally illiterate
- that the viability of public education is increasingly subject to question and challenge especially in the great cities of this nation
- that one in five children in the United States grows up in poverty
- that in a nation which is 12 percent African-American and 84 percent white, there are more African-American prison inmates and welfare recipients than white
- that if our planet were a village of 1000 people, 700 of us would be illiterate, 500 of us would be hungry,

and 60 of us would control half the planet's total
income

Public life happens outside the boundaries of family and
friendship (that is, private life), or is supposed to at any rate! Public
life is the social space where citizens and those who hunger and
thirst for justice must learn to register our claims competently and
persistently. It is not limited to what we call electoral politics. The
right to vote and even the act of voting are in actuality minimal
expressions of an authentic public life. The major crisis in the collective life of citizens of this country, namely the unraveling and
discrediting of genuinely democratic governance, is a crisis of public life.

Now consider typical associations with a word that surfaces
almost immediately when conversation turns toward public matters. The word is "politics." Adjectives strongly associated with that
word are "crooked," "corrupt," "untrustworthy," "wasteful," and
"ineffective." The frequency of such associations gives us a crude
but real measure of how we feel democratic governance is working
today. Low voter turnout for elections is another such measure.
These are indicators of the degradation that our experience of public life has undergone. For the most part public life in our time has
become equated with corrupted politics; if we attend to it at all, we
typically do so as disapproving but ineffectual spectators and com-
plainers.

It is, however, important that we temporarily suspend our con-
tempt for politics so as to be able to reflect critically on the political dimension of human existence in two particular ways. The first
is philosophical, even theological. Politics is about power. Power
names the capacity to have effects (which we associate readily with
power) and to receive effects (which we tend to associate not with
power but with its opposite). To exist is to have effects and to be
effected. To exist, therefore, is to be involved with power. If power
has come to be equated with domination in Western culture, it is
because our communal understanding and shared practice of power
as unilateral rather than a relational reality is distorted and distort-
ing. The conception of power as one–directional has distorted our
understanding not only of humanity but also of divinity. A unilateral
vision of power yields a world view populated by rugged individual-

ists who need nothing from other persons and owe them nothing, and an immutable and impassable God who cannot change or be affected by others.

Our second gloss on politics is historical, requiring that we retrieve an important bit of our Western cultural heritage. Politics is about how we behave together in the "polis," the city, or more inclusively, within whatever real-world community we exist. Politics in the Greek tradition was the name for the process whereby adult citizens worked out among themselves ways to provide for the common good. Building on Aristotle in this as in so much else, Aquinas characterized politics as a practice of moral virtue. In our time, care for the common good—the shared exercise of a truly public life— has been given over to politicians, to experts, and to people and institutions of great wealth and influence. As adults most of us have little or no real participation in the political choices which create the public life we experience. The common good today is whatever "they" make it. We may grumble about "politics" or tune in more seriously from time to time when particularly disgraceful or frightening events occur, but in truth we feel little potency to transform the way democracy works in our "advanced" society.

The state of politics in the contemporary United States is powerfully presented and explained in an important book entitled *Who Will Tell the People: The Betrayal of American Democracy* by William Greider (1992). It is a book that anyone concerned about our common public life should read. It is sobering because the citizens whose reflection we see in the mirror of Greider's text—ourselves—are typically ineffectual in the face of the wealth and power of those who move the public agenda, not in the service of the common good, but rather in pursuit of special economic and political interests. One of Greider's metaphors in fact is that our political system is like a two-way mirror between officeholders and those who elect them, a mirror which "reflects the warts and virtues back and forth between them" (1992, 16). In other words our elected officials are a reflection of us, as we are of them. For many of us, it is not a comforting thought. In Greider's words, if electoral politics "is infested by fools and knaves, where did they come from and who sent them?" (1992, 17).

Greider relentlessly details the breakdown in democratic structures in this nation, describing the dynamics by which citizen voices in government have been limited if not silenced by wealthy and powerful forces. And he does so with a clear sense of what is really at stake in the vitality of our common political life. In his words:

> Politics is not a game. It exists to resolve the largest questions of the society—the agreed-upon terms by which everyone can live peaceably with one another. At its best politics creates and sustains social relationships—the human conversation and engagement that draw people together and allow them to discover their mutuality. (1992, 13–14)

Politics is the place where citizens and people of faith who do not have access to great wealth and power must find our collective voices if we wish to affect the shape of our public life rather than simply be passive recipients of the effects of others.

An Example from Biblical Times

It may help to grasp the state of our public life by examining the same issue from another historical vantage point, one which is both strange and familiar to us. Approximately six hundred years before the birth of Jesus in Judah, the southern kingdom of Israel, our religious ancestors faced a time of crisis in *their* public life. A prophet stood up in the most sacred of his community's public places, the Temple in Jerusalem, to accost his people with the social devastation surrounding them. This is what he said:

> Thus says the LORD of hosts:
> Consider, and call for the mourning women to come;
>> send for the skilled women to come;
> let them quickly raise a dirge over us,
>> so that our eyes may run down with tears,
>> and our eyelids flow with water.
> For a sound of wailing is heard from Zion...
> Hear, O women, the word of the LORD,
>> and let your ears receive the word of his mouth;
> teach to your daughters a dirge,
>> and each to her neighbor a lament.

"Death has come up into our windows,
    it has entered our palaces,
to cut off the children from the streets
    and the young men from the squares." (Jer 9:17–21)

Those of us who inhabit America's cities today can readily identify with Jeremiah's social analysis. One of the growth industries in urban America is "home security"—alarms, private guards, and bars for our doors and windows lest death come up into them. How many city parents today would even dream of letting their children go play outside as they did in their youth? The squares, the public gathering places of our cities, have become killing grounds for young men, especially young African-American men, whose chance of being murdered before age twenty-five is one in five.

Notice Jeremiah's prescription for beginning the healing of Judah's body: Those women of the community who are skilled in dirges and lamentations must step forward to lead the people in collective grieving over the dying and over the fear which has arisen in their public life. Alas, Jeremiah's community not only failed to listen to the message, but they chastised the messenger. Utter defeat and captivity in Babylon were close at hand. Perhaps an acknowledgment of the great pain in our collective body, of our impotent complicity in it, and of our anxieties about our own well-being and that of all our children is required of us as a part of learning to bear the public choices central to the vocation named adulthood. Perhaps we are required to grieve before we can begin to address the real issues of public life in our cities, states, and nations. Perhaps the hearts, eyes, and voices of women must lead us through this necessary collective grief, thus opening the way to work for peace in our public life. But, having grieved, how do we create a base of influence through which we might increase the peace? For a plausible and hopeful response to this painfully pointed question, we return to the concept of mediating structures introduced in chapter 4.

Mediating Structures and Public Life

A sense of skeptical estrangement and helpless insecurity regarding our public life grows alarmingly even in democratic nations with highly developed economies. In *Democracy's Discontents*, political theorist Michael Sandel describes the core issues that underlie the pervasive estrangement from political structures so many citizens feel:

> The political parties…are unable to make sense of our condition. The main topics of national debate—the proper scope of the welfare state, the extent of rights and entitlements, the proper degree of government regula-tion—take their shape from the arguments of an earlier day. These are not unimportant topics; but they do not reach the two concerns that lie at the heart of our dis-content. One is the fear that, individually and collectively, we are losing control of the forces that govern our lives. The other is the sense that, from family to neighborhood to nation, the moral fabric of community is unraveling around us. These two fears define the anxiety of the age. (1996, 3)

To address this anxiety would mean establishing a measure of effectiveness in our ability to influence the political and economic forces swirling around us and reweaving the ethic of common con-cern that binds us together. In the words of Sheldon Wolin, we must nurture "our capacity for developing into beings who know and value what it means to participate in and be responsible for the care and improvement of our common and collective life" (1989, 139). Wolin refers to this capacity for seeking the common good in col-laboration with others as our "politicalness."

Where might citizens and people of faith stand in order to build the relationships and learn the skills necessary to develop our politi-calness—our ability to address political and economic decision-mak-ers respectfully, forcefully, and effectively? One answer is the myriad of voluntary associations including, but not limited to, congrega-tions, unions, community betterment groups, and neighborhood organizations—the "mediating structures" discussed in chapter 4.

Such associations constitute a "third sector," a zone within the over-all web of relationships not controlled by government or business. Within the mediating structures of our lives, which the philosopher Hegel first named "civil society," values and identities are sustained and transmitted. If the concern of government is order and the concern of business is profit, the concern of civil society is with ultimate meanings and values—the humaneness and holiness—underlying political order and financial dealings. Some orders and profits are just; others are not. In addition to the crucial moral learning that goes on in our families, we also learn to recognize the difference between good and bad order and profit in our churches, schools, and civic associations.

Taking mediating structures seriously will require that we call into question an image that Westerners take for granted in inter-preting our social world: We tend to think of our society as organized along lines very much like geological strata. When we use language like "upper class," "middle class," "lower class," and now "underclass," we're employing a background image of stratification. It is crucial that we recognize two things about this "stratigraphic" image of society: It suggests that (1) the basic structure of our society is a uniform and pervasive layering of socioeconomic statuses or classes, and (2) that a person's occupation, how he or she makes a living, is perhaps the crucial indicator of her or his prestige and life chances. It is precisely this assumption which contemporary socio-logical analysis calls into question.

While there can be little doubt that the options which come with one's occupational status have a significant bearing on one's life chances, there is another dimension to be considered. What we are likely to accomplish in our lives is never solely a function of our individual options, even those associated with our occupational earning power. The wealth or dearth of meaningful relationships which characterizes our lives also profoundly affects our life chances. Contemporary sociological research on the United States and other Western democracies makes it clear that two large-scale social trends have increased the complexity of society so greatly that the concept of social class in the sense of stratified occupational lay-ers systematically associated with increasing or decreasing life chances needs revision. These two realities, which reflect not merely economic forces but also national decision-making within our society, are our military institutions and involvements and our public welfare system. Both of these have altered the life chances of millions of citizens of our society so fundamentally that socioeconomic stratification in the classic sense (the "upper-middle-lower" geological strata model) no longer adequately describes our social structure. Our position in society is more complex than the familiar class-stratification model can account for by itself.

And there is another problem with the economic stratification model for society. It does not take into account the whole set of nonoccupational relationships that looms so large in our lives. This includes the complex pattern of ethnic and racial ties, religious affiliations, and a variety of local, regional, national, and international voluntary associations. These are the mediating structures introduced in chapter 4. Because these bonds often cut across lines of economic class, they also help to invalidate the picture of our social structure as a rigid stratification of occupational layers defining life chances.

The web of mediating structures into which people are born and which they further construct and modify is—along with their macrosocial status and options and microsocial bonds—a crucial determinant of their life chances. But how do mediating structures become a vehicle for renewed participation in public life?

Mediating Structures and Social Control

For almost every reader of this text the term "social control" will initially have restrictive if not coercive connotations. Some will perhaps think of the government, church, or the educational system's socializing people to take up and maintain constructive roles. For others the capacity of persons and groups to keep their behaviors within acceptable social limits may come to mind. For most of us, social control has overtones of coercive pressure exercised externally.

You may be surprised to discover, however, that in the classical American sociological tradition, social control referred to "the capacity of a social group to regulate itself according to desired principles and values" (Janowitz, 1975, 82). The concept was in fact propounded and developed by a group of social thinkers who insisted that an image of society as a collection of atomistic individuals pursuing their separate economic interests could not account adequately for society's actual functioning, and furthermore gave no acceptable basis for considering values or ethics. In their view, a social order based primarily on coercive external control rather than shared values was precisely the one that lacked adequate social control. How meanings change!

At the center of the classic understanding of social control is the assertion that legitimate differences of interest within a society are to be resolved by "persuasion, discussion, debate, education, negotiation, parliamentary procedure, diplomacy, bargaining, adjudication, contractual relations, and compromise" (Wirth, cited in Janowitz, 1975, 88). What all these modes of resolving differences have in common is their reliance on mutual communication. Properly understood and practiced, each of these forms of communication disavows the use of domination or coercion to resolve disagreements. They are exercises in relational power.

Social control in the classical sociological tradition was a way of speaking about having a public life. When sociologists first spoke of social control, they were not naming coercive or manipulative forces but rather the capacity of people to realize their values in the public arena, to have an effective public life. We reintroduce the classical approach to social control because it is crucial that Christian communities of faith be able to order our lives according to the fundamental convictions which give shape to our identity and, in doing so, to witness on behalf of those convictions to other persons and groups. That is, we must be capable of social control in the sense in which we have introduced it here. Put differently, communities of faith must have an effective presence in public life.

As we noted in chapter 2, the classic Christian texts having to do with power teach us that we are not permitted to lord it over others, but that we are called to exercise our influence with others "as one who serves." In other words, Christian witness in society must be persuasive rather than coercive, relational rather than unilateral. We must order our communal life and challenge others to collaborate with us to shape our public life according to the biblical values of justice and mercy, and we must do so in noncoercive ways through conversation, confrontation, and compromise. The historical Christian community understands very well what the classic social theorists were saying about social control. In fact, the notion of social control just presented springs partially from the Christian vision of the dignity of persons and how power ought to operate among us. Exercising social control in the classical sense—being a formidable public presence in the name of justice, mercy and love— is a hallmark of authentic Christian communities.

Social control as defined here occurs only when individuals, groups, and larger collectives can order their actual behavior in the world consensually according to their standards. Social control requires not only that congruence exists between what we profess as values and what we actually stand for in the world, but also that we arrive at our public stance and address others from it by means of mutual persuasion. Social control is one of the great challenges and possible achievements of social life. It reflects ideals of the historic democratic, Jewish, and Christian traditions. It can be arrived at and maintained only by persons working consensually and collabora- tively, patiently and tenaciously, in the public arena. It is particularly challenging amidst the extraordinary cultural pluralism of contem- porary Western societies.

Human beings attempting to pursue personal choices in iso- lation from the relational bonds of family, community, church, and the other associations which make those options viable and mean- ingful, imperil themselves and others. Good and meaningful choices require good and meaningful relationships. Nor can we regulate our lives according to our values apart from effective, mutual relations both within the groups to which we belong and between those and other groups. Personal and group integrity depend upon our capacity to maintain noncoercive mutual accountability within the web of our relationships. This is true at the micro-level of face-to-face interaction (e.g., the inner life of small faith communities) and at the macro-level of political life (e.g., the public life of small communities).

The Public Life of Faith

The Christian community is committed to the well-being of all the children of God. We stand under the extraordinary and chal- lenging mandate to love our neighbor as our self, that is, to value and work for the life chances of all our sisters and brothers as we value and work for our own well-being. Human well-being entails not only personal opportunities but relational bonds. To promote justice, mercy, and love within society and history is not only to stand for decent opportunities for every person, but also to defend and strengthen the mediating structures—the families, congregations, neighborhoods, schools—which alone make such opportunities meaningful.

The Christian community is called by its scripture and later traditions to link persons together into one body, into networks of mutual concern and involvement. We are to nurture a world of shalom, of right relationship, within human history. The Christian community is one of many forms of mediating structures. While our faith does indeed have a personal dimension, it is never a private matter, something just between us and God. Neighborliness is for us not merely a perfunctory or secondary obligation but a sacred one. Christian existence is fundamentally communitarian—or social—in nature. Whatever affects social relationships is relevant to the body of Christ in history, which, as Paul reminds us, we are and of which we are members.

Finally, the Christian community is under biblical obligation to order our internal and our public life on behalf of the reign of God in history. We are to contribute to the exercise of democratic social control by participating effectively in public life on behalf of God's intentions for history as mediated through our tradition. Biblically speaking, these intentions may be reduced to this: God desires a social world characterized by justice and mercy. We must stand for these values by conducting our internal ecclesial affairs and our relations with the rest of the world in noncoercive fashion. It is our community's vocation to be a credible and powerful presence in the real world on behalf of justice and mercy, to be a community animated by love, and to embody those qualities by conducting our relationships in such a way that we exercise our influence without lording it over others.

Our concern for the realization of these goods is not subject to cultural or socioeconomic boundaries. The inclusivity of the social vocation of the Christian community of faith forbids any form of dominance of one group of siblings over another. Coercive power is not to be our way of exercising influence, neither inside the community of faith nor outside it. To speak plainly, the presence of racism or sexism within the community of faith is an especially egregious violation of the biblical vision. Communities of faith cannot be credible witnesses or effective agents against such systemic evils unless we have an unambiguous commitment to uproot them from our own ecclesial life. Such realities always have political implications, especially when we recall that politics simply names the realities of power in communal decision-making. But this does not allow us to dismiss such matters as "merely political" rather than religious. It is precisely our inherited religious understanding of right relationships as just and merciful—as loving—that requires that we strive to free our own ecclesial and civic politics of racism and sexism.

For those who live on society's periphery, the exodus from slavery to peoplehood is a root metaphor for the kind of history they can make when they respond to Yahweh's promise. The exodus event has been paradigmatic for the poor and marginalized in Latin America, for the African-American and other cultural communities in exile in North America, indeed for many of those dispossessed by the abuse of power. Middle class people, however, have a different experience and face a different challenge if we are to stand in common cause with our sisters and brothers on the margins of the dominant society in making history today. Communities of faith located in the middle class inevitably read both their newspaper and Bible from the perspective of that location. Lest their faith become captive to their culture and society, middle-class SCCs must be prepared to put their received versions of faith and culture under creative suspicion, to test them in conversation with the social realities of marginalized others and the true otherness of biblical, especially prophetic, texts. Unless people of faith in the middle class are feeling unsettled by both of these, we are missing the point of both.

Walter Brueggemann popularized the expression "prophetic imagination" to remind us that the prophets imagine reality differently from most others, that is, they have different images for interpreting life. They know that God has intentions for the world that would redeem human experience in ways we can barely imagine. They feel deeply that "something else might be the case." They do not, of course, speak the language of practical theology as we have articulated here, but they speak their own version. They feel the contrast between what is the case (cultural and social analysis) and what should be the case (faith analysis). And their essential passion is that what *could* be the case *should* be the case. Why? Because that is the word their God has communicated to them. Abraham Joshua Heschel insists that while the prophets are moved by their own indignation at injustice in their cities and their nation, their real power comes from elsewhere. Their relationship to Yahweh is so profoundly personal that they feel the world with Yahweh's own feelings. At that point the mystical and political are one. Then the prophet arises to warn us, in Heschel's words, that "a people may be dying without being aware of it; a people may be able to survive yet refuse to make use of their ability" (Heschel, 1962, xii). Such is the public burden of the prophets of Israel.

Of the many christological titles given to Jesus (son of David, son of man, son of God, and even the title of Christ), perhaps only two belong to the historical life of Jesus, prophet and teacher. Both of these have been so eclipsed by later titles that they all too often do not shape our collective sense of who the Christ is and what it means to follow on the Way. Jesus called the something else that might be the case "the Kingdom of God" and urgently pressed for its realization with his life. In the mutually critical conversation between culture and faith called "practical theology," which we outlined in chapter 4, small Christian communities open themselves to the searing and inspiring words of Jesus and his prophetic predecessors and successors. In doing so, they find these surprising, challenging, consoling words addressed to them about the world as it is here and now. Through faithful and informed conversation with scripture and world, communities of faith not only retrieve those words but find our communal imaginations challenged and revitalized in the recovery. Such communities are called to transformative action in the name of justice and mercy and then to reflection upon both the effectiveness and the religious significance of that action. Can anything be said about specific biblical challenges to today's communities of faith? We want to approach that question first by way of an additional text from the prophet Jeremiah, and then by considering Catholic social teaching on the "preferential option for the poor."

As we noted above, Jeremiah's people did not heed his cry for public mourning and renewal, and near the end of the sixth century B.C.E., God's chosen people saw their political kingdom broken into pieces. The leaders and most of the people were sent into exile; the

Babylonian captivity was upon them. In this time of pain and ban-ishment, the Word of God came to this community from Jeremiah once again, now in the form of a letter to the exiles. Through his messengers, Yahweh Sabaoth, the God of Israel, said to all of the exiles deported from Jerusalem to Babylon:

> Build houses and live in them; plant gardens and eat what they produce. Take wives and have sons and daughters; take wives for you sons, and give your daughters in mar-riage, that they may bear sons and daughters; multiply there, and do not decrease. But seek the welfare of the city where I have sent you into exile, and pray to the LORD on its behalf, for in its welfare you will find your welfare. (Jer 29:5–7)

Biblical scholars note Jeremiah's realism. This may be a less-than-ideal situation, but the captives should be practical enough to make the best of it. They are not to rail against and resist the cap-tors. They are to make a fruitful and constructive existence in the city of Babylon, where they have come against their will. Surely this is the voice of prudence. But Jeremiah does not stop with prudent advice for survival in a strange land. He proceeds to make the astounding claim that the well-being of those in exile against their will and the well-being of those who dominate them are one: "[I]n its well-being you will find your well-being." Not only must we seek the well-being of those who devastated and now dominate us, but we must pray to God for their well-being. The Word of God sees one world where partisan eyes can only discern divisions.

The Word of God sees a world without tribal hatreds, a world without strangers. Imagine the surprise of a vanquished, grieving, angry community on hearing that they must seek a world of justice and mercy on behalf of the very ones who have inflicted such dis-ruption and torment upon them, that upon the shalom of "their" city hangs the shalom of God's vanquished people.

To speak plainly, many members of small communities of faith find ourselves today like our sisters and brothers in captivity in Babylon so long ago, exiled within a public life that affronts our deepest religious instincts and seems impervious to our influence. To make a decent living and raise a healthy family in safety is no small concern today. Contemporary urban life is particularly dangerous territory. We are well aware of individuals and communities suffering from burnout and "compassion fatigue" after attempting courageously to address these stark and sobering social realities. As urban exiles, many people of faith are challenged and inspired by Jeremiah's letter. He voices a repeatedly experienced truth about the social and religious vocation named community: Without a commitment to public life, the inner life of small communities of faith cannot thrive. We have no choice but to seek the well-being of our city and to pray to God on its behalf; like Jeremiah's people in Babylonian exile, the urban dwellers of today have no individual well-being in isolation from the well-being of our cities. The same religious reality of course also holds for nonurban residents.

The Hebrew word in Jeremiah's letter which we are translating "well-being" is shalom. To seek the shalom of our society has a specific biblical meaning. Shalom is the peace which emerges when human beings are in right relationship with themselves, their neighbors, the earth and all its creatures, and God. In the Jewish world view (which was, of course, the world view of Jesus), "right relationship" has two characteristics: justice and mercy. Right relationship means the proper balance of justice and mercy called for by the real social circumstances within which we find ourselves in our time and place. What right relationship requires of us at any given moment is a judgment call which God has left to us. In making it we must exercise both religious discernment and practical wisdom. The fundamental challenge to adult citizens and people of faith is to exercise our influence and allow ourselves to be influenced by others as we seek relationship (that is, shalom) in the give-and-take of public life. True shalom emerges only from the practice of relational power.

In sociological categories the well-being of a people has to do with the life chances which they inherit as a result of their social location—their opportunities for health, education, safety, decent housing, nutrition, and so on. Jeremiah's exhortation reminds us that one group's life chances cannot be divorced from those of others. To cooperate in the improvement of the opportunities of others for a decent, peaceful life is to improve our own chances for such a life. Can middle-class people of faith exiled in the cities and suburbs of the United States and other Western nations, witnessing daily to

events which break our hearts and demoralize us, open our lives to
the words of Jeremiah? Can we risk crossing racial, denominational,
and class boundaries in order to seek the shalom of the troubled and
gifted places in which we find ourselves?

The Preferential Option for the Poor

Responding to situations in South America, contemporary
theology has developed the concept of the "preferential option for
the poor" to frame the deeper instincts of God's justice and mercy
in both testaments. The last judgment scene in Matthew's gospel is
perhaps its quintessential expression. What we do for the hungry,
the sick, the despondent, and the imprisoned expresses our relationship with Jesus Christ. For the sake of our collective salvation,
then, we must be mindful of painful social facts regarding the life
chances of all members of our society. A preferential option for the
poor does not mean that they are loved more than everyone who is
not poor. Parents of a sick child do not love that child more than
their healthy children when they give major attention, energy, and
care to that child's recovery. But they want the sick child to be
healed. That can be translated to something like this at the macrosocial level: There is an acceptable level of human resources and
self-determination below which no one should be forced to live.
Those below that level have first call on our energies and resources
until as far as possible they are sisters and brothers with us in decent
levels of human living.

There is a remarkable power for transformation in the middle
class—for seeking the well-being of the city and especially those marginalized by poverty—if we can learn to speak as citizens and people
of faith in a collective voice that transcends race, class, and denominational membership. If the middle class wants a better world for our
children, there are serious reasons for binding coalitions with the
poor and with others of good faith who have already made such coalitions. An equal love must move in both directions. In solidarity with
the poor and with those marginalized for other reasons (gender, race,
sexual orientation), we are far more likely in our ongoing critical conversation to imagine vigorously that something else might be the
case, that some different city might hold a finer world for tomorrow's
children, that in the well-being of the city we shall find our own well-

being. That is so largely because in real and sustained relationships with others whose world views and interests differ from our own, we inevitably find that new possibilities for life, for the shalom of our common world, emerge for consideration. When the time is ripe, those possibilities become the basis for collective action. Communities who turn themselves toward political and economic injustice because scripture has accosted them are no less subject to paralysis than an individual facing those challenges. If anything they may be in more jeopardy because their ongoing conversation with scripture inexorably calls them to the actual life circumstances of people in the social world we share. The usual individual processes of numbness and denial regarding racism, sexism, and other systemic injustices will inevitably be subverted by an ongoing shared reading of scripture. Reading the Bible well with sisters and brothers in community but without adequate channels for collective action is like periodically reopening a wound. That wound is our complicity with an unjust social order and the effects it has on the life chances of others as well as our own and our children's. We repeatedly feel a kind of learned helplessness in the face of a public life gone wrong.

Seeking the well-being of the city—our cultural and social world—is not simply a private matter of being better individuals, although that is of course our responsibility as well. Nor is it simply a matter of gathering with others to share our faith in conversation and worship and to support one another personally, although no authentic community is imaginable without such fellowship. Genuine Christian community also requires that we face together as persons of faith the true state of our social body, our public world.

When Christian communities seek the well-being of the city, they will inevitably be led into the arena which we have here called public life, that is, into the places where racism, sexism, and political and economic injustice are perpetrated and must be confronted. As noted above, the prophets of Israel were no strangers to this arena. Jesus and those who preceded him had to deal with the sociopolitical arrangements of their time and place. The life of Jesus was in fact taken by the demonic use of unilateral power by Roman public officials. A Christian community which does not find itself in the public arena has lost its way. And the dominant culture of individualism and consumerism offers endless inducements for us to lose our way in the addictive pursuit of material possessions and endless self-actualization.

It is precisely in the public world that communities of disciples of Jesus Christ must be prepared to lose our lives in order to find them, as we seek the well-being of all God's people. Christians on the margins of all societies (the "people of the base") understand this readily and find great hope in it. (It is they, in fact, who gave birth to the movement of small Christian communities around the world, a movement which is now struggling to construct an authentic form in North America and elsewhere.) It is a terribly difficult task, however, for communities of faith that find themselves in the middle-class sector of a highly individualistic, materialistic, and relatively prosperous culture such as ours.

Past experience has convinced us that continued reading of biblical texts in an isolated fashion is a prescription either for a retreat into a private, "spiritualized" ("me and God") reading of scripture or for guilt-driven, nonsustainable plunges into charity. If we read the scriptural texts alone—whether as individuals or isolated communities—they will simply break our hearts. A larger solidarity is required of us if we are to be accosted but not demoralized by scripture's powerful word. Individuals and isolated communities of faith cannot face events in the public arena alone with any measure of hope. Even communities which face these events in solidarity with others must expect moments of desolation. But our historical community of faith emerged and continues to exist out of the remarkable conviction that captivity in a strange land is not the last word, that there is a new form of life available to those who are prepared to lose their lives by going on the way, that in seeking the well-being of the city, we will find our own well-being. That seeking and finding will require small communities of faith to become part of a larger mediating structure, one whose overriding agenda is the common good of the larger community.

Broad-Based Community Organizations: Seeking the Shalom of Public Life

Near the end of his book on the state of political participation in the U.S. today, William Greider describes what in his judgment is the most promising effort to reclaim true citizen involvement in the decisions of public life: the community organizations which together make up the Industrial Areas Foundation (I.A.F.) network. For the past thirty years in several English-speaking countries, citizens and people of faith based in their congregations, civic associations, and labor unions have been rebuilding public life by patiently reconstructing and revitalizing democratic discourse and action across the barriers of race, class, and religion. In San Antonio, a city where people of one culture formerly functioned as menial laborers for those of another, a vibrant, bicultural civil society has emerged. In East London, civic participation has begun to function within a mix of cultures and religions that those who founded the mother of parliaments could never have imagined on English soil. In Baltimore, the largest scholarship-and-jobs-incentive program in the U.S. has been created for public school students. In New York, communities of homeowners, including many former public-housing residents, exist where politicians and experts said they never would. In New Orleans, the specter of racism is being addressed directly in open, public discourse between African Americans and whites. In Johannesburg and Soweto, democratic institutions are being painstakingly created to fill the civic vacuum left in the wake of apartheid. In the city and suburbs of Chicago, the urban heart of the United States, a metropolitan-wide, multicultural citizens' organization has been created on a scale never before attempted.

Broad-based organizations are centered in local congregations of all sizes, economic classes, races, cultures, and denominations, as well as in other forms of community groups and associations. By coming together in a larger form of solidarity, they cross racial, denominational, and class barriers as they seek the well-being of their social worlds in committed and effective ways. These organizations, which are large mediating structures composed of many institutions, create a new and sustainable base of power for change in which citizens and people of faith may involve themselves. As the examples in the preceding paragraph indicate, they have a remarkable track record in affecting the public life of their communities in concrete and creative ways. They have made the views of their member institutions known and affected public decisions in matters ranging from public education reform to affordable housing, from community policing to economic development, from public health and sanitation to minimum-wage levels.

The overarching goal of broad-based organizations is to empower citizen leaders to develop a common agenda for reconstructing the crumbling physical and social infrastructure of their communities, while strengthening their integrity and diversity. Their commitment is to institutional change at the most profound level: how citizens make those collective, public decisions regarding economic development, education and training, housing, and so on, which will determine the future well-being of their communities. One respected I.A.F. leader, Reverend Johnny Ray Youngblood of St. Paul's Community Baptist Church in East Brooklyn, speaks about the vision and power of broad-based organizing in these words:

> There are some mandates loose out there. Thou shalt run. Thou shalt move. Thou shalt buy more alarms. Thou shalt put wrought-iron gates over thy windows. Thou shalt buy a gun. Thou shalt change schools. Thou shalt change cities. But we come from our own Mount Sinai and have another mandate before us. The mandate is East Brooklyn Congregations. The mandate is I.A.F. The mandate is, thou shalt organize. Thou shalt organize, disorganize, and reorganize. Contrary to popular opinion, we are not a "grassroots" organization. Grass roots grow in smooth soil.
>
> Grass roots are shallow roots. Grass roots are tender roots. Grass roots are fragile roots. Our roots are deep roots. Our roots are tough roots. Our roots are determined roots. East Brooklyn Congregations has fought for its member institutions' existence in the shattered glass of East New York, in the blasted brick and rubble of Brownsville, in the devastation of central Bushwick. Our roots are deep in this city. (Freedman, 1993, 322)

A defining characteristic of I.A.F. organizations is their plurality. Within these organizations African Americans, Hispanics, and Asian Americans collaborate as equal partners with Americans of European decent in the pursuit of justice for members of all faiths and cultures. Within these organizations Jews, Christians, and

Muslims seek the well-being of their cities. Within these organizations women and men share leadership, authority, and public roles. Within these organizations city dwellers and suburbanites come together to face issues which neither can address alone. Within these organizations citizens and people of faith from urban and rural communities collaborate on matters of mutual interest. Within these organizations conservatives, moderates, and activists seek common ground, refusing to allow ideological differences to become political divisions.

In the collective experience and shared vision of the citizen leaders and professional organizers who have willed the remarkable network of I.A.F. organizations around the world into being, and sustained and renewed them in the face of the divisive economic pressures and cultural tensions of our time, there resides a precious storehouse of practical, political, public wisdom. These women and men comprehend something that only those who have ventured beyond the confines of private concerns into the arena of public life can know. They understand what it means in practice to make common cause with people of other races, religions, and classes in seeking the well-being of the larger civic communities to which all belong. They have celebrated exhilarating victories and experienced the sacrament of defeat in public life, and they have done both in the company of former strangers now become fellow citizens.

These organizations exist to amplify the sorrowful voices of individuals so that they will be heard throughout the community. They become stages from which choruses of lamentation can rise up from the devastated and demoralized public life of their communities. Through their own experience, they have come to understand what biblical scholar Walter Brueggemann means when he says that only when grief moves from private pain to appropriate, disciplined, public expression does true empowerment of people of faith and citizens begin and the dream of a revitalized public life arise anew. Within these painstakingly built and constantly developing organizations, people who for the most part have no access to great wealth or power are learning how to evoke the cries of individuals, to see that they are heard in the corridors of real power, and to look to themselves as responsible and effective agents in the reconstruction of public life in their communities. Broad-based community organizations seek the shalom of their communities.

Small Communities in Broad-Based Community Organizations: A Work in Progress

In *Dangerous Memories*, we suggested that small communities of faith could be thought of as mediating structures between households and the larger institutions of our social world. Subsequent experience has led us to another view: A small community of faith alone is simply too small to play the role of mediating structure. We have become convinced that in order to play this crucial intermediate role in the lives of their members, small communities must invent forms of solidarity with other groups and institutions which share their vision of a world of shalom.

We close this chapter by describing one such experiment. Since 1992 a number of small faith communities have involved themselves in the creation of a broad-based organization, like those described above, in metropolitan New Orleans. Called The Jeremiah Group, the organization has at the time of this writing about thirty member institutions, including a small faith community. Like the other members, the small faith community pays dues to the organization (typically $1000 per year), sends some of its members to local and national training to learn how to create and move a public agenda, engages in public actions which engage elected officials and other power brokers in the community, and participates in the collective leadership of The Jeremiah Group.

The small faith community that belongs to The Jeremiah Group is composed mainly of white, middle-class, well-educated Catholic professionals. Through their membership in this broad-based organization they now have the opportunity to forge strong public relationships with members of African-American churches, congregations of other predominantly white denominations, and the Jewish community of New Orleans. In this mixed multitude they experience not only shared social analysis and action, but common worship woven from the diverse strands of many cultural heritages. Thus the diversity of a broad-based organization gives participating congregations and communities a viable solution to a vexing and chronic problem: In such organizations white churches do not have to recruit black members or vice versa in order to be in real relationship with diverse others. Those relationships take place not primarily within congregations or communities but rather within the larger organization in which they participate together.

As we write, the small community of The Jeremiah Group is involved in campaigns to address a number of critical public-life issues in metropolitan New Orleans, including a desperately under-supported public education system, a shortage of affordable housing for low- to moderate-income families, and the lack of living-wage jobs within an economy too closely tied to tourism. These are indeed public issues, and in working within a broad-based organiza-tion which is initiating constructive action in response to them, the SCC of The Jeremiah Group is learning what it means to have a public life as a vital complement to their continuing inner life. Following one of the organization's first large public actions, the mayor of New Orleans was quoted in press coverage as follows: "I'm touched when I look out and see white and black, brown and yellow, Jew and Gentile, Protestant and Catholic, old and young, Uptown and Downtown, together in one place for one purpose." New Orleans SCC members were in that number when the mixed multitude of saints mentioned by the mayor came marching in to seek his commitment to become an ally of The Jeremiah Group in seeking the shalom of the city.

In addition to the public work of the organization, members of the New Orleans SCC have also been part of an ongoing public conversation called "Calling the Question of Race," in which lead-ers of The Jeremiah Group gathered over two years across racial lines for dialogue and study about how race and racism distort both the public and personal lives of citizens of Western cultures. Those participating in these ground-breaking (and anxiety-provoking) conversations thus far have commented on how rare it is for blacks and whites to address these matters head on and together in the context of ongoing relationships in an interracial collective. It is precisely such ongoing public relationships which participation in a broad-based organization makes possible for SCCs.

Closing

Old testament scholars like Norman Gottwald and Walter Brueggemann, and New Testament scholars like Bruce Malina, Gerd Theissen, and Wayne Meeks, help us understand why anthropology and sociology illuminate the nature of the people of God. To become "a people" is to become a system, with cultural, economic, and political characteristics and peculiarities. We think it is fair to say that while the body of Christ is many things and subject to interpretation under many rubrics, it is also and always a "body politic" that interacts with other political bodies. Not to acknowledge that is to miss a very critical feature of our life in Christ.

Our corporateness does not absorb our personal relationship with God. Our public activity does not replace our personal prayer. All the rituals of the marketplace will never displace the table of Eucharist. The personal "I" that prays and organizes never stops being a unique "I" of incomparable worth, even as it never stops being an "I" whose identity is forever emerging from relationships with God and with each other. Each of us is truly one and many, and we pray and act in both ways.

Communities of faith exist within particular historical circumstances and are called to transform them in accordance with the intentions of our Creator as these are mediated to us through our religious traditions. A biblical reading of those intentions is clear: God wants a world of shalom, of peace. But, as rabbinic Judaism has traditionally taught, God cannot bring such a world into being without human partners committed to the fulfillment of creation through the practice of *mitzvot*, actions on behalf of mercy and justice. The transformative action to which the descendants of Moses and Jesus are called by their ongoing critical conversation with culture and society has both a practical and a public character. What we are learning from the wedding of Christian communities and broad-based community organizations holds promise for a creative explosion of the public life of SCCs in the United States. We are equally certain that SCCs have signal contributions to make to effective and sustainable community organizing in the name of justice and mercy. No doubt there are and will be other ways for small communities of faith to have a public life. We offer this example as the most powerful instance we know of small communities committing to an intentional public presence.

SCCs can be true to their name only by venturing into the public arena to build relationships with diverse others in the pursuit of the common good of the larger community. If they fail to do so, they are actually religious support groups. Having risked engagement in public life, they must return to reflect, pray, and converse as people of faith about what they have experienced in exercising their politicalness. If they fail to do so, they are actually activist groups. Authentic SCCs must develop both their inner and their public life. And so we have come full circle: Seeking consensus, utilizing conflict, and developing leadership in their inner life and an ongoing commitment to seek the shalom of the city in their public life are the two crucial moments in the one conversation that constitutes small Christian communities. The price for such conversation is the willingness to risk what we already have and what we already know. The possibility which inevitably attends that risk is conversion.

7

Formation:
The Value of Community

Why Formation?

A grant from Lilly Endowment, Inc., made possible a very extensive study of "Small Christian Communities in the U.S. Catholic Church." In this book we have referred to what we have learned from that research. The phenomenon of SCCs has not been studied with the same empirical thoroughness in any other country in the world. A second grant supported the dissemination of that research. The dissemination process has been in the mode of practical theology, not just giving out data, but eliciting from participants concrete pastoral responses to this development in American Catholic culture. The dissemination process culminated in a national assembly of more than six hundred SCC leaders and members. They were addressed by experts on SCCs, American society, and the U.S. Catholic Church. They deliberated about what they heard around tables of eight. They questioned and challenged the experts and each other. They fellowshipped over meals and broke the bread of Eucharist together. They developed an agenda for the movement of SCCs among Roman Catholics in the United States. A report on that agenda is included in our final chapter.

One recommendation on that agenda was that SCCs would be well served by attention to formation needs. For example, it would be beneficial to have a forum for dialogue between the grassroots experience of Catholic life in SCCs and broader issues in Catholic church life. Further, the mixed blessings of abundance in many parts of American life prevent sustained attention to critical human need from being an instinctual point of reference. But SCC members are also people with the potential to facilitate significant responses to the claims of the reign of God. Better resources could be a great boon. Critical issues around leadership and mission deserve attention. For all of these reasons, in this chapter we discuss formation requirements.

A Shifting Personnel Picture

In an earlier time, many men and women preparing for a vocation in the religious life began with a one- to four-year high-school postulancy program. After high school, they experienced a very intense novitiate year, followed by a scholasticate of three to four years; many went on to earn graduate degrees after that. Men preparing for the priesthood studied at the minimum four years of philosophy and four of theology. This education was not only intellectual and academic; it was also a profound socialization into the culture of the church and the charism of a religious order. The leaders and teachers of the U.S. Catholic Church came almost entirely from these ranks.

In Catholic culture, the word *community* has carried a lot of weight. The value of community in Catholicism owes much to the community experience of monks and innumerable religious orders. The faithful following of Jesus is always communal in character. When Jesus invites, "Follow me," the follower immediately belongs to the twelve, or the seventy-two, to an itinerant community, or a resident house-church community.

In 1965 there were 215,000 religious in the U.S; by 1999 the number had dropped to 106,000, with only 3.5 percent of the membership forty years old or younger. There are two growing but still underdeveloped responses to this new kind of church, one which now lacks priests to staff the country's 19,000 parishes and which no longer has the huge presence of religious women and men in hospitals, schools, orphanages, and the like.

Parishes

In the 19,000 parishes in the U.S. Catholic Church, the number of nonordained women and men offering pastoral ministry half-time or more jumped from 21,560 in 1992 to 29,146 in 1997, while the number of priests dropped from 30,955 in 1992 to 27,154 in the same period. The number of nonordained pastoral agents now outnumbers the ordained. Large parishes that once had three to five priests now have one. Many small parishes do not have a resident pastor or have been merged with several other parishes under one pastor.

The education of lay Catholics for ministry takes place in diocesan programs and in some fifty graduate programs in Catholic colleges and universities, which currently enroll double the number of seminarians in theology. But salaries for these lay ministers are often insufficient to retain them, especially when there are families to support. And the kind of financial resources that funded the education of seminarians and religious have not been made available generally for the education of the new company of lay leaders and pastoral agents.

It is noteworthy that, while there are 19,000 parishes in the country, there are no fewer than 40,000–50,000 small church communities. Twenty-five years ago there was a mere handful of SCCs, largely continuations of the 1960's "underground church" communities. For the sake of the church, these communities need informed leadership and superb resources. We believe, with Karl Rahner, with whose words we opened this book, that communities will play a formative role in the becoming of the twenty-first century Catholic Church.

Religious Virtuosi

In *Pathways to Re-Creating Religious Community*, Patricia Wittberg borrows the category of "virtuoso" from the sociology of Max Weber. Even Weber was a little apologetic for the aristocratic sound of the word. Weber and Wittberg are trying to name the fact that in all social organizations there are a few people who are more dedicated, more passionate, more concerned, more imaginative, more adept, more committed, more generous, and more available. At a time when religious life was often spoken of as the "way of perfection," which left other callings somewhat below that, many Catholic "virtuosi" joined a religious order. With Vatican II comes the recognition that all people are called to the same perfection, and marriage is also a charism of perfection.

Wittberg cites, from Illana Friederich Silber's *Virtuosity, Charisma, and the Social Order,* five characteristics of virtuosity (1996, 228–29):

1. It is a matter of free choice,
2. It entails a "search for perfection, an extreme urge to go beyond everyday life and average norms of achievement,"
3. This search for perfection is carried on in a disciplined, systematic fashion,
4. It implies a double standard of religious practice, a division between the virtuosi lifestyle and that of the average adherent, and
5. It is based on achievement, not inheritance.

When Wittberg begins her chapter on the religious virtuoso, she says this "simply refers to someone who desires more than the 'church on Sunday' level of devotional practice which satisfies others among the faithful" (Wittberg, 1996, 19). This seems to fit the sort of people who become members of SCCs. They hunger for more than is available in the normal parish, the sorts of things that the papal exhortations after the Synods identified as small groups with interpersonal relationships, in pursuit of a better world, meaning, the reign of God.

It seems a reasonable guess that some of the Catholic virtuosi who would have become priests or members of religious orders now find their way into SCCs.

In Catholic colleges and universities and in many diocesan programs, we are developing formation for lay women and men who will play, and indeed are already playing, major leadership and pastoral roles in the church. The formation needs to be broader and far less expensive (or with more scholarships and financial aid available), but it is under development.

Here we name our judgment about the kinds of formation that SCCs deserve, for the sake of the reign of God, and for the good of the church.

Formation! Formation! Formation!

The easier part of this chapter is to name the kinds of formation that will add to the strength and vitality of small church communities. The challenge, which we can name but not instigate by merely writing about it, is to institutionalize formation, by which we mean using resources and organizations already available, and development and institutionalization of new ones, to proffer SCC formation programs at many levels.

Five areas require focused formational attention:

1. Developing Skills in Situational Analysis

Reading the signs of the times is not easy. "Mere" common sense often misses deeper currents and causal impulses that need to be understood. On the other hand, members of SCCs are not called to be practicing academic sociologists. In between is the wise practitioner, who has at hand a methodological approach that is easily manageable and suited to group use.

In earlier parts of this books we recommended such approaches to situational analysis as *Reinventing Theology* by Ian Fraser and *Social Analysis: Linking Faith and Justice* by Joe Holland and Peter Henriot.

Many broad-based community organizations have developed models for situational analysis that can be used by people without any specialized education. For example, the Industrial Areas Foundation (IAF) and the Pacific Institute for Community Organization (PICO) both work largely with congregations in a city. Social analysis—though those words may not be used—often takes place in house meetings where people from the same area can speak to local issues. Then in larger meetings, concerns are brought from multiple house meetings and congregations. Out of this discernment the larger organization's agenda emerges. Many of these processes could be useful in the life of SCCs.

What a community chooses to address can reflect its mission within the community or beyond. Within community, concerns might be prayer life, ritual, or the use of scripture. Concerns beyond the community's immediacy may be the parish, the school system, or the city.

In all of this, scale is important. A small church community is not church on the scale of a diocese or a parish. It has to sense how much agency it really has. If a task is of critical importance and a community's scale is too small to tackle it, one of the possible options is to connect with other communities, that is, to organize.

These and other models of situational analysis are a community's reading of the world, which will be in dialogue with their reading of the Word. Both must be read accurately.

A more complex dimension of situational analysis is the task of understanding what is happening to us in our society, our culture, and our nation, and how all of that impacts upon what is or could be the reign of God. This level of theological reflection needs expertise. It perhaps needs a place as well, either a location where events of this nature can take place and where deliberation can be shared; or perhaps something akin to an online *Journal of Practical Theology for SCCs.*

2. Retrieving the Original Scriptural Voices

Albert Schweitzer once said that if you want to get to know someone, get the person to write a life of Jesus. You won't learn much about Jesus, but you'll learn a lot about the person writing the life! It is so simple, for reasons that are natural and easy to understand, to read Jesus from a thoroughly contemporary bias, instead of biases that belonged to a rural Jewish peasant in first-century Palestine.

Many Christians envision a sort of generic Jesus assembled from the four gospels, with little awareness of how differently the Markan community, for example, experienced and interpreted Jesus than the other three gospel communities, or the Pauline community. Jesus and the writings about him come from two thousand years ago. They are in a language that Americans do not speak—so we choose a translation. They come from a Mideastern culture that differs hugely from our own. What's more, our contemporary political and economic systems shed little light on first-century Palestinians. In a word, it is often very difficult to let scripture speak here and now with its original voice, its original cadences, and its original intent. To hear another person accurately, we must let the words mean what they mean to the speaker, even if we do not agree with those meanings. To get cultural information about an ancient time, it will help me hear the text differently than I would otherwise have heard it.

For example, many of us know the story of the "widow's mite," as it is often called. Few of us remember that the passage just preceding it is Jesus' scathing critique of the lifestyle of the scribes and his insinuation that they support that lifestyle by devouring the estates of widows. Scribes were notorious for taking unconscionable fees as executors of estates (women were not allowed to be executors). So, while Jesus surely praises the widow who gave all she had and then had nothing left, he also laid a heavy critique upon the social system responsible for her drastic state.

Stressing the importance of contemporary biblical scholarship, in 1994 the Pontifical Biblical Commission issued a document, *The Interpretation of the Bible in the Church*, underlining the critical importance of learning from biblical scholarship (*Origins*, January 6, 1994, 23/29). "The study of the bible," the text says, "is the soul of theology....This study is never finished; each age must in its own way newly seek to understand the sacred books."

The challenge is obvious. Most Catholics will have neither the background nor the time to read the Bible in light of contemporary exegesis. But we who are writing this text both teach scripture to lay men and women and know that many people can gain access to helpful materials, generated out of excellent scholarship, without becoming scholars. They become trained readers. The issues that SCCs must face include finding effective interfacings between trained readers of the Bible and the ordinary readers who make up most small group members. Although there are lectionary-based publications for SCCs, it is our judgment that thus far none of them does an adequate foregrounding based in contemporary biblical scholarship. They are solid discussion starters and promoters, but they seldom search for the analogous connection between meanings in the original text and meaning in our contemporary context.

This problem is addressed with great insight in a rather technical book, *Biblical Hermeneutics of Liberation: Modes of Reading the Bible in the South African Context*, by Gerald West. West describes the Centro de Estudos Biblicos (CEBI), founded in Brazil, to address the interface between scholarship and ordinary readers.

The common factor that unites the work of CEBI is a Bible reading methodology. The reading methodology of CEBI involves three crucial commitments: first, a commitment to begin with reality as perceived by the organized base; second, a commitment to read the Bible in community; and third, a commitment to socio-political transformation through Bible reading....The second commitment highlights the importance of a communal reading of the Bible. No one can read the Bible alone, there must be a search for consensus in the group. This commitment binds biblical scholar and ordinary readers together. While the base has in the past been suspicious of intellectuals this is not necessarily the case. Biblical scholars are continually being "called" by the people.... The biblical scholars who are part of the CEBI process are committed to doing biblical studies with and from the perspective of the poor and oppressed. (West, 1991, 216–17)

The church in South Africa felt the same tensions and has opted similarly to address them with the Institute for the Study of the Bible (ISB), whose primary aim "is to establish an interface between biblical studies and ordinary readers of the Bible in the church and community that will facilitate social transformation" (West, 1991, 219). This process has four components (West, 1991, 220):

1. A commitment to read the Bible from the perspective of the South African context, particularly from the perspective of the organized poor and oppressed.
2. A commitment to read the Bible in community with others.
3. A commitment to read the Bible critically.
4. A commitment to individual and social transformation through contextualized Bible study.

We believe that a very important formation need in our own context is for an institutionalized response that reflects the social realities of U.S. life. SCCs do not currently have access to any such resources.

The formula for critical SCC theological reflection, if one can put it that way, is:

- read the world together in community,
- read the Word together in community,
- decide together in community what the dialogue between world and Word requires,
- then do it.

It is the season, the *kairos* in biblical language, for a new U.S. version of CEBI and ISB.

3. Integrating SCCs into Church Structure and Organization

In the U.S. Catholic Church, there has been explicit support in Hispanic ministry for SCCs. There is not, however, any format for SCCs and the institutional church to receive each other's experience and hear and address each other's concerns. We believe there is a need for a format of speaking and listening, but not one that lets the grassroots exploration of SCCs get hijacked.

Second, there is no format for integrating SCCs into parish structure that incorporates them into regular parish bodies without prejudice to parishioners who are not members of an SCC. We think that the broad experience of the National Alliance for Parishes Restructuring into Communities (NAPRC) has the widest experience in this regard and should be a key player in any such deliberations. This is prime theological reflection.

The catechumenal potential of SCCs in a parish could be a centerpiece for the kind of structure we suggest is needed. Major tasks of an RCIA team could be done by SCCs to which the parish can delegate many of the tasks of catechumenal formation. While there are certainly doctrinal components to RCIA formation, the process is primarily one of being socialized into Catholic life and Catholic culture, into the Catholic people of God. The North American Forum for the Catechumenate and the North American Forum for Small Christian Communities are already engaged in this conversation, which is a natural for NAPRC as well. Maybe this is enough. Or maybe it would benefit from a theological home.

4. Developing SCC Leadership and Mission

We dealt with leadership at length in chapter 5. Here we only add that formation in leadership would be a gift not only to SCCs but to the larger church. We have learned from broad-based community organizing that in the processes of situational analysis and in dealing with the public, leaders emerge or are created who probably would not have come forth otherwise. Similarly, people in SCCs discover gifts they didn't know they had, like presiding over a community's prayer, facilitating good conversation, organizing events, and so on. SCCs have the potential for being schools of leadership for the larger church world. Yet given what the research has uncovered about the SCC tendency to rather flat leadership, organized leadership formation would greatly assist the continuing development of SCCs in the U.S. Catholic Church.

Any social group that is successfully doing what it claims it wants to do almost certainly has a clear sense of its mission. Arriving at mission clarity—a calling—and effectively implementing it will not happen without effective leadership, accessing all the gifts and wisdom of the community to that end.

5. Encouraging Ongoing Conversation between Grassroots SCC Experience and Systematic Theology

Although SCC members may not think of themselves as theologians, whenever they name their personal and social experience, examine that experience in the strong light of their faith, and then act on it, they are functioning as practical theologians at the grassroots level. Given the size of the SCC phenomenon in a church searching for its future forms, systematic theological reflection upon grassroots theological reflection is a potential gift. It would be important that, when SCCs hear from academic theologians about ecclesiology or christology, they will recognize their story. This would be an extraordinary activity of the church and gift to the people of God—like "home schooling," an ecclesial in-house learning that people do together.

Whether this needs to happen in a physical place or during a regular structured gathering is immaterial at this point. But it is not likely to happen without responsibility for its orchestration being lodged somewhere.

Closing

We have tried to give full attention to both the gathered life and the sent life in SCCs in the U.S. Catholic Church. As Americans with religious commitment, our cultural context makes it easier for us to gather as support groups than as action groups. The recent research by Robert Wuthnow, cited in chapter 2, indicates that one out of every four Americans belongs to a small group, and nearly always the groups are support or special interest groups. We also sense the need for patience and nurture in regard to mission, as SCCs spring up in the U.S. Catholic Church. Socially expressed public concern for issues by religious groups is not a natural instinct in this culture. Though frequently misunderstood, "separation of church and state" is a buzzword in American society. Tax exemption is removed from any religious group that publicly, as a community, takes political positions. One advantage of marginal SCCs is that they can speak and act without being structurally identified with the institution.

It is too early to guess what church historians will say a century from now about the global phenomenon of small Christian communities. While they have come into existence on all continents and in many sizes and shapes, they are still a minority of the total number of Catholics. We believe that these communities have the yeast-like quality that Jesus mentions, the ability to leaven a mass.

In sociological categories, the phenomenon of small Christian communities is not technically a movement, for there is no kind of central organization that directs it. But there are similarities. The SCC phenomenon is neither a fully structured institution nor a totally free-form reality. It is a complex blend of the hunger for the charism of *communitas* and the need for the good order of *societas* discussed in chapter 3. The SCC movement has observable patterns to it, while including many variations. We have suggested, for example, that compared to now familiar church structures like parishes within dioceses, all SCCs fall outside the norm to a degree. Within the phenomenon of SCCs, some are clearly organized in a more mainstream and some in a more marginal form. Some SCCs fit comfortably within the rhythms of parish life as we now know it; others emerge largely as a critical response to strongly felt short-comings of today's parish.

It is important to remember that, like all social structures, the church arrangements we now take for granted were once creative social inventions to make church available to people who needed it in new circumstances. Consider, for example, the creation of subur-ban parishes in residential settings of a kind which had never existed before the 1950s, or the parish administered by a lay woman or man in the current decade (parish life coordinators in parishes without a resident priest-pastor). This kind of creativity always requires stretching of ecclesial structures. It is helpful to remember that present structures needing to be replaced probably caused some stretch marks when *they* first came into play. Today's solution to unmet needs within the community of faith has a way of becoming tomorrow's problem, as *communitas* and *societas* continue their tense, creative dance. If SCCs become more and more integrated into the formal structures of church, then in time they too are likely to become the foil for an as yet unimagined transformative movement of the Spirit in due season.

In the meantime, the work of those who care about the move-ment of small Christian communities is to nurture the conversation which we have endeavored to describe in these pages in both its inner and public forms. Participation in that conversation, as we have insisted from our opening pages, cannot be separated from the experience of conversion. For members of authentic small Christian communities, the fuse is indeed always laid to some annunciation.

8

National Priorities:
Where Do We Go from Here?

The most recent gathering of small Christian communities in San Antonio, Texas, was an important event for shaping and animating the future of SCCs in the U.S. Catholic Church. This was the third such national gathering, but a first in the emphasis placed on engaging in theological reflection on SCC experience in dialogue with U.S. Catholic culture and U.S. civil culture.

With generous funding from Lilly Endowment, Inc., to the Loyola Institute for Ministry in New Orleans, a team of six theologians and a team of five sociologists and one anthropologist had planned and carried out the extensive research on small communities described earlier in this book. Therefore our theological reflection in San Antonio was experientially grounded in the real experience of SCCs: which people belong to communities, what they do, what difference they make, what their concerns are, and so on.

At the conclusion of the gathering, Dr. Patricia Killen invited those present to respond to this question: "What has your experience at this convocation over the past three days meant to you in terms of your understanding of this gathering and your small community as church?" One of the participants observed, "I leave with the hope that we can create a national agenda for the public life of the SCCs."

The Scripture reading from Qoholeth, chapter 3, is a reminder that for all things there is a time or a season. In Greek there is a distinction between clock time (*chronos* time) and the exquisite sensibility that knows just when something should be said or should happen, when it's exactly the right "season" (*kairos* time). To us, it is highly plausible that for small Christian communities in the U.S.

190

Catholic Church, this is a *kairos* moment. The convocation was the first occasion that communities gathered at a national meeting specifically to engage in theological reflection together in the mode of practical theology. This was a deliberate choice of the three organizations that co-sponsored the convocation, and also of the multiple national organizations that were consulted in the process and participated in a preconference planning meeting. The convocation was about "Where do SCCs go from here, based on our experience and based on our sense of the life of the Catholic Church?" The outcome of the convocation was a framing of seven national priorities for SCCs for the proximate future. Here we link the priorities with remarks that SCC members and leaders made in response to Patricia Killen's "exit question." Many reflections about the convocation corroborated the general concerns of the priorities.

New National Priorities

1. *We recognize our need for better networking of SCCs among ourselves and among our national organizations.* Often we do not know much about what other communities are doing. What's more, multiple national organizations that have interests in the life of small Christian communities are not regularly in touch with each other. That lessens our possible impact upon the life of the Church.

"This experience," wrote one participant, "has affirmed my belief in SCCs and the importance that these groups have in the church. Now is the challenge.... Time is of the essence. Networking and support will be critical." That networking was the number one priority is significant. But there were reservations voiced, often that SCCs not lose their grassroots prophetic energy and insight because of too much organization too soon. "I favor a national organization, but only for networking and sharing resources. We must always remember the grassroots base of SCCs." Another participant said, "I hope that organizing organizations do not attempt to put too much structure in place. It's too early in the movement for that."

Some SCCs do not feel connected beyond their own group. One member wrote that "I was very comfortable with the security, comfort, and closeness of my SCC before this convocation, but now I see a lack of [connection] and a sense of isolation—we have held ourselves exclusive and separate without feeling responsible for the larger church." This reflects the feeling of others that local net-working is as important, or maybe more important than national networking. One move might be to rethink the structure of current national and diocesan organizations so that what already exists can better mobilize strengths, energy, and people.

SCCs recognize the need for better organization for two reasons. Communities themselves need to be in better touch with what goes on in other communities. But also, better organization will help SCCs make a larger, more focused contribution to church and society. But they do not want organization that will diminish the freshness and zest of what they do and are.

2. *We need to forge a much better relationship, a partnership of equals, between Hispanic/Latino SCCs and Anglo SCCs.* One of the strengths of the convocation was that its location in San Antonio made possible a large Hispanic participation. Simultaneous translation was available at the gathering. Some workshops were in Spanish, and some small group processing was in Spanish. Most of the planning came from the Anglo side, although we benefited greatly from input from the Mexican-American Cultural Center.

What became clear in the conference is that there are significant differences between Hispanic and Anglo SCCs, but that many of these are rich and complementary differences. It was also clear that most of us from the Hispanic or the Anglo experience are not very informed at all about the other's experience. Where we go from here must proceed from a genuine partnership of equals. For that to happen, we need explicit commitments and concrete strategies for communication and collaboration. It won't "just happen."

The implementation of the SCC priorities needs some kind of organization at the national level—in this instance, to work systematically with Hispanic and Anglo leaders to devise how this partnership will be formed and energized. It will not be easy. One participant wrote that "I saw quite a gulf between Anglos and Hispanics in church loyalty and identification. It will make it hard to work together." This second national priority speaks of a serious desire to foster deeper collaborative relationships between Anglo and Hispanic communities, and other ethnic communities as well.

3. *It is important to gain the support of bishops and pastors.* A strong and healthy tension exists between the desire for relationships

between SCCs and the hierarchy, and the desire not to have grass-roots insights and energies of small church communities co-opted.

SCCs know that they can thrive more easily when bishops and pastors are supportive. They are deeply aware that they are already church and want to be significantly connected. But, along with the desire for organization, SCCs do not want to lose their initiative "from the base." One participant felt that SCCs might not yet be clear enough on their own agenda to present themselves formally. "I also see a large number of small community agendas raised by a lot of speakers and spokespersons. I suspect that these different agendas will probably interfere with any unified presentation which could be made to governing bodies such as the National Council of Bishops."

Some of the hopes expressed are for connection with local pastors and local parishes. Another participant said that "our communal experience of faith, life, and mission are an expression of church but needing a deeper connecting to the larger gathered church." Still another expressed hope for the realization that SCCs are "part of a larger parish community, diocese community, national community, and international community." "The experience ignited in me," said another, "a desire to communicate the importance of SCCs...to church leaders, pastors, priests, etc."

There are similar points raised here with the notion of greater national organization. One participant put it very well: "The last three days have been energizing, affirming, and stretching. It reminds me of the delicacy of *balance* we need to keep growing/reaching out and the richness, indeed the essence of personal and communal spiritual growth, which grassroots individual small Christian community nurtures."

The Catholic Church currently experiences this dialectic in a number of areas: the debates between Cardinals Kasper and Ratzinger concerning the local and universal church, and between bishops and Catholic universities in the context of *Ex Corde Ecclesiae;* no organization, in fact, can be healthy without the dialectic between *societas* and *communitas.* It must be said that even among SCCs there are differences in their individual tilt towards *societas* or *communitas* in self-understanding.

It would be our hope that there be somewhere a "home" for the kind of ongoing theological reflection that this dialectic requires to keep the *ekklesia* healthy and open.

4. *We need to learn better ways to organize SCCs for our public life.*
This involves both emphasizing peace and justice issues, and learning how to forge links with already existing social justice groups.
This priority comes from the recognition, voiced at the convocation
and addressed earlier in this book, that while social concern is a high
value, actual social involvement is low. Most of us know this and do
not quite know what to do about it. The research upon which much
of the convocation's theological reflection was based made clear that
SCCs find it easier to address their inner life (gathered) than their
public life (sent), many of the reasons for which are rooted in the
individualism in U.S. culture.

In addresses that helped nourish the convocation's theological
reflection, Robert Bellah spoke about the impact of individualism,
and Patricia Killen addressed the need to focus more intentionally
in the relation of faith to the larger world and its needs. Those two
presentations helped give many people some words with which to
recognize and name their own desire to address social issues more
effectively, at the same time acknowledging the difficulty they experience in doing so.

What captured our imagination at the convocation was naming
the power of small groups to help transform the world, especially if
it becomes a more conscious intention and if there is the organization to support it. One person just returned from an SCC experience
in Latin America said, "I'm recently back in the country—and am
very happy to see SCCs on the increase. These communities have
[transformed] and will continue to transform people who can transform the Church—and the world." Another said that "there is so
much power (in the good sense or the bad) in this movement. If we
respond and move forward, we are truly capable of changing not
just our own lives but the general world."

There is a sense in many of the comments that, as regards faith
and public life, SCCs may be in a position to do what the larger
church isn't doing yet. One participant wrote that "once we do it
well in small groups perhaps we could teach the larger church community and help all Christians understand the radical message of
the Gospel and its call for social justice." We wonder, for example,
what might have been or might yet be the outcome if U.S. bishops
were to ask SCCs to take their pastoral letters on justice and peace,
and run with them!

5. *We need to learn how to welcome youth and young adults into small Christian communities.* At the convocation, one had only to look around to see that young adults were few in number. They are also relatively absent from the church, given their numbers in the general population. On the other hand, the young adults that were at the convocation were very vocal, very present, and deeply appreciated and heard. The appetite for more young adult Catholics in SCCs was clearly whetted by their outspokenness. They also formed one of the caucuses in which national priorities were discussed and formulated.

We would simply say that this is one more example of a priority that is less likely to be addressed effectively without some kind of ongoing effort to evoke continuing theological reflection and provoke strategic pastoral implementations. Just wanting more young adults in this important ecclesial development will not make it happen. Their essential gifts must be identified, invited, and welcomed.

6. *We must attend to the need to communicate Catholicism's rich tradition.* The research on SCCs indicates that the major energizing religious practice is correlating scripture and lived experience, and that while there is no negativity toward the doctrinal tradition, it does not enter regularly into SCC processes. In his keynote address, Scott Appleby praised the recovery of scripture in ordinary Catholic life, but challenged SCCs to do a better job of accessing tradition in their dynamics.

This emphasis resonated with many present. Some felt it important, for example, to remember that SCCs were the first form of organized church life. "What happened during this gathering for me was a passing of the tradition of the early church communities to the present day: that we are empowered to renew the real Church of Christ by giving voice to the SCCs." Appreciation of the tradition and the power of SCCs to evoke fidelity to Vatican II is reflected in the observation that "when we begin to reflect on Church tradition in small Christian communities the changes will come—and how our culture and worldview dialogue with our tradition will transform us....[T]he emphasis will shift on what we need to teach and what we pass on, our knowledge of Vatican II and what it meant in the context of our tradition. The power we have as lay people will become known and Vatican II spirituality will finally have a chance to emerge."

7. *We need to pay attention to leadership needs of SCCs if they are to continue to flourish and respond well to these national priorities.* This need, strongly expressed at the convocation, is clear. The research on SCCs indicated clearly that community leadership formation deserves serious attention.

A major presentation by Evelyn and James Whitehead developed a relational, participative model for thinking about leadership. One of the workshops, conducted by a young adult leader, Rick Boesen, presented a structural model that had all members of a small community in one of three standing committees: the Inner Life Committee, the Public Life Committee, and the Practicalities Committee. This spreads leadership out in focused ways. Patricia Killen's reflections also suggested how important it is that someone have the skill to lead communities in theological reflection. Here again, it would help to have a national organizational help in naming specific resources, and in keeping this need to the forefront of SCC consciousness.

The Context for these Priorities

The third national convocation of small Christian communities, entitled *Small Christian Communities, Church, and Society: From Paul's Corinth to North America*, took place August 1–4, 2002, at St. Mary's University in San Antonio. The more than 600 participants included twelve other nations (Canada, Mexico, Brazil, Australia, Tanzania, Uganda, Kenya, Nigeria, Ireland, England, Scotland, and Sweden). This was the third conference cosponsored by Buena Vista or BV (National network of Small Christian Communities), the National Alliance of Parishes Restructuring into Communities or NAPRC, and the North American Forum for Small Christian Communities or NAFSCC (diocesan personnel responsible for SCCs).

A grant from Lilly Endowment, Inc., to the Loyola Institute for Ministry at Loyola University, New Orleans, had provisions for a national conference for the dissemination of research on "Small Christian Communities in the U.S. Catholic Church." Instead of having a parallel national conference, Loyola made grant resources available to a joint effort with BV, NAPRC, and NAFSCC and was a participant in the convocations' planning.

We also invited and profited from advice and collaboration from the following groups: the National Pastoral Life Center, RENEW International, the Marianist Lay Network of North America, the Mexican-American Cultural Center, the Leadership Conference of Women Religious, the Conference of Major Superiors of Men's Religious Orders, the Religious Brothers' Conference, the National Association of Diocesan Directors of Campus Ministry, the National Catholic Ministry Association, the National Confederation of Catholic Youth Ministry, the National Black Catholic Caucus, the Council on Pastoral Planning and Council Development, the National Federation of Priests' Councils, the National Association of Deacons, and representatives from three NCCB/USCC secretariats: Family, Laity, Women, and Youth; Doctrine and Pastoral Practices; and Evangelization.

What gave definition to this third national gathering was the decision to structure the entire meeting on the model of practical theology: a mutually critical conversation between interpretations of faith experience and interpretations of the larger world. The goal of the conversation was to generate strategies for Christian life. The Lilly-funded study of SCCs was a primary document interpreting the faith experience. The structure of the convocation was developed through extended critical conversation between Michael Cowan and Barbara Fleischer on the practical theology side, and the Coordinating Task Force, consisting of two representatives from each of the three sponsoring organizations, and Bernard Lee, who was project director for the research. The task force members were Nora Petersen (coordinator) and Hector Rodriquez from Buena Vista; Carolyn McKenzie and Reverend Michael Schneller from the National Alliance for Parishes Restructuring; and Sister Nancy Fisher and Carlette Chordas from the North American Forum for Small Christian Communities.

The coordinators and facilitators for the convocation were Michael Cowan and Barbara Fleischer, both from Loyola, New Orleans. Music and liturgy were coordinated by Waldemar Perez and David Kauffman. David Kauffman coordinated a program of new music written especially for small Christian communities by some of this countries leading composers (including himself): Derek

Campbell, Jaime Cortez, Kate Cuddy, Marty Haugen, Bob Hurd, and Lori True. A Marianist grant commissioned the new music. The beleaguered yet effective conference planner was Terry Wessels of TM Conference Services, and the coordinator at St. Mary's University, the convocation site, was Hector Rodriguez.

Finally

We have been intimately involved in trying to understand and track the development of small Christian communities over more than twenty years. During this time we have seen extensive growth in both the numbers of SCCs and the networks and organizations that support and service them. What continues to amaze us is that these communities have sprung up all over the world, and without any kind of central promotion and encouragement. They have "just happened," in very different ways in very different places—but nearly always as a meeting between scripture and experience, or put differently, between faith and life. The seven priorities just named sound very much like a national agenda for SCCs in the U.S., and this is a new development.

In the U.S. Catholic Church, SCCs have been very loosely connected or organized. But perhaps it has just taken us time to grow up, as our numbers suggest we have done. We agree with the priorities and support the emergence of some kind of national center to serve *ekklesia* through the explicit nurture of SCCs and the concerns they have identified.

Bibliography

Arbuckle, G. *Refounding the Church*. Maryknoll, N.Y.: Orbis, 1993.

Avery, M., Auvine, B., Streibel, B., and Weiss, L. *Building United Judgment*. Madison, Wis.: Center for Conflict Resolution, 1981.

Azevedo, M. *Basic Ecclesial Communities in Brazil: The Challenge of a New Way of Being Church*. Washington, D.C.: Georgetown University Press, 1987.

Banks, R. *Paul's Idea of Community: The Early House Churches in Their Historical Setting*. Grand Rapids, Mich.: Eerdmans, 1980.

Baranowski, A. *Creating Small Faith Communities: A Plan for Restructuring the Parish and Renewing Catholic Life*. Cincinnati: St. Anthony Messenger Press, 1988.

Barreiro, A. *Basic Ecclesial Communities: The Evangelization of the Poor*. Maryknoll, N.Y.: Orbis, 1982.

Barrett, L. *Building the House Church*. Scottsdale, Penn.: Herald Press, 1986.

Bellah, R., Madsen, R., Sullivan, W., Swidler, A., and Tipton, S. *Habits of the Heart*. Berkeley: University of Claifornia, 1985.

Boyt, H. *Commonwealth*. New York: Macmillan, 1989.

Branick, V. *The House Church in the Writings of Paul*. Wilmington, Del.: Glazier, 1989.

Briggs, K. *Holy Siege*. New York: Harper Collins, 1992.

Brown, R. *Priest and Bishop*. Paramus, N.J.: Paulist Press, 1970.

Brueggemann, W. *The Prophetic Imagination*. Philadelphia: Fortress, 1978.

Buber, M. *The Legend of the Baal-Shem*. New York: Schocken, 1969.

Camille, M. *Image on the Edge*. Cambridge, Mass.: Harvard, 1992.

Cobb, J. *Christ in a Pluralistic Age*. Philadelphia: Westminster, 1975.

Cowan, M. and Lee, B. *Conversation, Risk, and Conversion: The Inner and Public Life of Small Christian Communities*. Maryknoll, N.Y.: Orbis, 1997.

Crosby, M. *House of Disciples: Church, Economics, & Justice in Matthew*. Maryknoll, N.Y.: Orbis, 1988.

Emerson, R. *Essays and Lectures*. New York: Library of America, 1983.

Fisher, R. and Ury, W. *Getting to Yes*. Boston: Houghton Mifflin, 1981.

Freedman, S. *Upon This Rock*. New York: Harper Collins, 1993.

Geertz, C. *Local Knowledge*. New York: Basic Books, 1983.

Greider, W. *Who Will Tell the People: The Betrayal of American Democracy*. New York: Simon & Schuster, 1992.

Hanson, P. *The People Called*. San Francisco: Harper & Row, 1986.

Heschel, A. *The Prophets*. San Francisco: Harper & Row, 1962.

Janowitz, M. "Sociological Theory and Social Control." *American Journal of Sociology*, 81 (1), 1975.

King, P., Maynard, K., and Woodyard, D. *Risking Liberation*. Atlanta: John Knox, 1988.

Kleissler, T., LeBret, M., and McGuinness, M. *Small Christian Communities: A Vision of Hope*. New York: Paulist, 1991.

Lee, B. *The Future Church of 140 B.C.E.* New York: Crossroad, 1995.

Lee, B. and Cowan, M. *Dangerous Memories*. Kansas City: Sheed & Ward, 1986.

Lee, J. *Marginality*. Minneapolis, Minn.: Fortress, 1995.

Lohfink, G. *Jesus and Community*. Philadelphia: Fortress, 1984.

Macneice, L. *Collected Poems*. London: Faber and Faber, 1979.

Malherbe, A. *The Social Aspects of Early Christianity*. Philadelphia: Fortress, 1983.

Malina, B. and Rohrbaugh, R. *Social-Science Commentary of the Synoptic Gospels*. Minneapolis, Minn.: Fortress, 1993.

Meeks, W. *The First Urban Christians: The Social World of the Apostle Paul*. New Haven, Conn.: Yale University Press, 1983.

Meier, J. *A Marginal Jew*. New York: Doubleday, 1987.

Metz, J. *Faith in History and Society*. New York: Crossroad, 1980.

Myers, C. *Binding the Strong Man*. Maryknoll, N.Y.: Orbis, 1988.

Overman, J. A. *Church and Community in Crisis: The Gospel According to Matthew*. Valley Forge, Penn.: Trinity Press International, 1996.

Owensby, W. *Economics for Prophets*. Grand Rapids: Eerdmans, 1988.

Pelton, R. *From Power to Communion: Toward a New Way of Being Church Based on the Latin American Experience*. Notre Dame, Ind.: University of Notre Dame Press, 1994.

Phillips, K. *Boiling Point*. New York: Random House, 1993.

———. *The Politics of Rich and Poor*. New York: Random House, 1990.

Quigley, W. "The Rich Get Richer: So What?" *America*, June 17, 1996.

Rahner, K. *The Future of Man and Christianity*. Chicago: Argus, 1969.

Reich, R. *The Work of the Nation*. New York: Alfred Knopf, 1991.

———. "The Secession of the Successful." *The New York Times Magazine*, Jan. 20, 1991.

Riesman, D. *The Lonely Crowd*. New Haven, Conn.: Yale, 1950.

Rorty, R. *Philosophy and the Mirror of Nature*. Princeton, N.J.: Princeton, 1979.

Sandel, M. *Democracy's Discontent*. Cambridge, Mass.: Belknap, 1996.

Sarason, S. *The Psychological Sense of Community*. San Francisco: Jossey-Bass, 1974.

Schillebeeckx, E. *Christ the Sacrament of the Encounter with God*. New York: Sheed & Ward, 1963.

Schreiter, R. *Constructing Local Theologies*. Maryknoll, N.Y.: Orbis, 1985.

Schüssler Fiorenza, E. S. *Discipleship of Equals: A Critical Feminist Ekklesia-logy of Liberation*. New York: Crossroad, 1993.

———. *In Memory of Her: A Feminist Theological Reconstruction of Christian Origins*. New York: Crossroad, 1983.

Schwartz, B. *The Battle for Human Nature*. New York: Norton, 1986.

Sennett, R. *The Fall of Public Man*. New York: Vintage, 1970.

Simons, R. *Competing Gospels*. Alexandria, Australia: E. J. Dwyer, 1995.

Slater, P. *The Pursuit of Loneliness*. Boston: Beacon, 1970.

Theissen, G. *The Social Setting of Pauline Christianity: Essays on Corinth*. Philadelphia: Fortress, 1982.

———. *Sociology of Early Palestinian Christianity*. Philadelphia: Fortress, 1978.

Tracy, D. *The Analogical Imagination: Christian Theology and the Culture of Pluralism*. New York: Crossroad, 1981.

———. *Blessed Rage for Order*. New York: Seabury, 1979.

———. *Plurality and Ambiguity*. San Francisco: Harper & Row, 1987.

Vandenakker, J. *Small Christian Communities and the Parish*. Kansas City: Sheed & Ward, 1994.

Veling, T. *Living in the Margins*. New York: Crossroad Herder, 1996.

Waetzen, H. *A Reordering of Power: A Socio-Political Reading of Mark's Gospel*. Minneapolis: Fortress, 1989.

Westley, D. *Good Things Happen: Experiencing Community in Small Groups*. Mystic, Conn.: Twenty-Third Publications, 1992.

Whitehead, E. "Leadership and Power." In Cowan, M. (ed.) *Leadership Ministry in Community*. Collegeville, Minn.: Liturgical Press, 1987.

Whitehead, E. and Whitehead, J. *Community of Faith: Crafting Christian Communities Today*. Mystic, Conn.: Twenty-Third Publications, 1992.

Wolin, S. *The Presence of the Past*. Baltimore: Johns Hopkins, 1989.

Wright, F. *Northern Ireland: A Comparative Analysis*. Dublin: Gill and Macmillan, 1987.

Wuthnow, R. *Sharing the Journey*. New York: The Free Press, 1994.

Appendix

Networks, Organizations, and Resources

Buena Vista

P.O. Box 5474

Arvado, CO 80005-0474

Phone: (303) 657-9428

Buena Vista began as a network for parish-based communities, but is now much more inclusive in membership. Newsletter. Annual meeting. Resource materials (print and video).

International Office of RENEW

1232 George Street

Plainfield, NJ 07062

Phone: (908) 769-5400

Post-Renew was developed especially for groups that want to continue as communities when the formal Renew Program has been completed, but its videos and printed resources have a wide application. SCC resources (videos and printed materials).

Latin American/North American Center for Church Concerns

215 Hesburgh Center—Kellogg Institute

University of Notre Dame

Notre Dame, IN 46556

The Center fosters church dialogue between Latin America and North America, with a special concern for SCCs. It has sponsored two international consultations and published *International Papers in Pastoral Ministry*.

Loyola Institute for Ministry

P.O Box 67

6363 St. Charles Avenue

New Orleans, LA 70118

Phone (800) 777-5469

The Institute for Ministry is conducting a three-year research project on Small Christian Communities in the U.S. Catholic Church, funded by Lilly Endowment, Inc. The Institute also offers a master's degree in Pastoral Studies, with a focus in Basic Christian Community Formation.

Ministry Center for Catholic Community

540 N.E. Northgate Way, Suite 141

Seattle, WA 98125

Phone (206) 763-6222

Lay founded and lay led, this Center has SCC resources for scripture, for liturgical seasons, and for topics of special interest.

National Alliance for Parishes Restructuring into Small
Communities

310 Allen Street

Dayton, OH 45410

Phone: (937) 256-3600

Fax: (937) 256-7138

naprcoffice@ameritech@net

The Alliance serves parishes that work to include SCCs as a structured form of parish life. The printed resources and videos are useful in wider contexts as well.

National Forum for Small Christian Communities

Office of Evangelization

1935 Lewiston Drive

Louisville, KY 40216

Phone: (502) 448-8581

Intended originally as a network for diocesan personnel with
responsibilities for nurturing SCCs, this group still functions that
way, but is also open to a more inclusive membership.

North American Conference of Associates and Religious

Bon Secours Spiritual Center

1525 Marriottsville Road

Marriottsville, MD 21104

Fax: (410) 442-1394

This recently formed organization facilitates networking and communication among associate communities sponsored by religious
congregations and publishes a quarterly newsletter.

Quest: A Reflection Booklet for Small Church Communities
The Pastoral Department for Small Christian Communities
467 Bloomfield Avenue
Bloomfield, CT 06002
Phone: (860) 243-9642, Fax: (860) 242-4886

Sunday by Sunday
1884 Randolph Avenue
St. Paul, MN 55105-9934
Phone: (800) 232-5533

This lectionary-based liturgy of the Word, prepared for small Christian communities, offers a 4-page guide for each Sunday, available by subscription. Published under the auspices of the Sisters of St. Joseph of Carondolet.